From H

By Daniel Melehi

©December 2023

# Contents

# Introduction

Welcome to the book "From Hoarder to Order: Decluttering Your Mind and Environment." This book has been specifically written for individuals who have been grappling with hoarding disorder and are seeking guidance to overcome it. Hoarding disorder is a complex mental health condition characterized by the excessive accumulation of possessions and the inability to discard them, regardless of their value or usefulness. It affects not only the physical space but also the mental and emotional well-being of individuals, as it often leads to feelings of overwhelm, distress, and isolation. In this book, we will explore the various aspects of hoarding disorder, including the signs and symptoms, the consequences it can have on an individual's life, and the emotional and psychological impact it has on their well-being. We will delve into the root causes of hoarding, understanding why it manifests in certain individuals, and explore effective therapeutic approaches to address the disorder. The journey From Hoarder to Order requires motivation and commitment, which we will help you develop throughout the book. We will introduce different therapies such as Acceptance and Commitment Therapy (ACT), Cognitive-Behavioral Therapy (CBT), and Dialectical Behavior Therapy (DBT) that have shown promise in treating hoarding disorder. We will also explore mindfulness techniques that can aid in managing the overwhelming emotions often associated with decluttering. The second part of the book focuses on the practical steps of decluttering your physical environment. We will guide you through the process of sorting and categorizing your belongings, creating organizing systems, and implementing maintenance routines to sustain a clutter-free lifestyle. We will provide strategies for letting go of sentimental items and for managing paperwork and documents, which are often major contributors to clutter. Dealing with cluttered spaces is a challenge, but we will provide practical advice on how to address it effectively. From creating functional living spaces to implementing cleaning and sanitizing practices, we will help you transform your living environment into a peaceful and organized sanctuary. Furthermore, this book acknowledges the importance of addressing hoarding behaviors at the source. We will explore methods to overcome emotional attachments to possessions and build healthy coping mechanisms to prevent relapse. Building a support network and seeking professional help will also be discussed as key components of the recovery journey. We understand that hoarding disorder not only impacts individuals but also their relationships and families. We will provide insights into navigating hoarding within these dynamics and offer guidance on how to support a loved one struggling with hoarding disorder. Lastly, we will focus on fostering self-compassion and acceptance throughout the process. Our goal is to help you embrace a clutter-free life and experience the freedom and peace that comes with it. Throughout this book, we encourage you to engage actively with the content, reflect on your own experiences, and take steps towards positive change. Remember that your journey towards order begins with the decision to seek help and make a commitment to a clutter-free life. Now, let's embark on this transformative journey together, as we explore the path From Hoarder to Order.

# Chapter 1: Understanding Hoarding Disorder

Hoarding disorder is a complex mental health condition that affects many individuals, causing them to accumulate excessive amounts of possessions and struggle with letting go of these items. In this chapter, we will delve into a comprehensive understanding of hoarding disorder, exploring its definition, characteristics, and underlying causes.

# DEFINING HOARDING DISORDER

Hoarding disorder is a persistent difficulty with discarding or parting with possessions, regardless of their actual value. This condition goes beyond normal clutter or excessive collecting. People with hoarding disorder experience intense distress and anxiety at the mere thought of getting rid of their belongings, often leading to extreme clutter that impedes their ability to use living spaces for their intended purposes.

# CHARACTERISTICS OF HOARDING DISORDER

Hoarding disorder is characterized by several key features. These include:

## Excessive Acquisition:

Individuals with hoarding disorder tend to acquire and accumulate a vast number of items, often far beyond what they can reasonably use or store.

This behavior stems from an intense need to possess and control objects, which provides them with a sense of comfort and security.

# Difficulty Discarding:

One of the defining characteristics of hoarding disorder is the extreme difficulty individuals face when it comes to discarding their possessions. They attach strong sentimental value to items, perceive potential usefulness in nearly everything, and fear that they may need discarded items in the future.

# Severe Clutter:

Hoarding disorder leads to excessive clutter and disorganization within living spaces, making it challenging to navigate or use rooms as intended. Clutter may cover furniture, countertops, and even block doorways, creating hazardous and unsanitary conditions.

# Emotional Attachment:

People with hoarding disorder often develop deep emotional attachments to their possessions. These attachments serve as a source of comfort and security, providing a sense of identity or serving as a connection to the past. Letting go of items feels like letting go of a part of themselves.

# CAUSES OF HOARDING DISORDER

Hoarding disorder is influenced by a combination of genetic, environmental, and psychological factors. While the exact cause remains unknown, studies suggest a genetic predisposition, abnormal brain functioning, and traumatic experiences as contributing factors.

# TREATMENT APPROACHES

Effective treatment for hoarding disorder involves a multidimensional approach, addressing both the individual's mental health and the physical clutter in their environment. In the upcoming chapters, we will explore various therapies and strategies that can help individuals overcome hoarding disorder and reclaim their lives. Understanding hoarding disorder is the first step towards finding effective solutions. By gaining insights into its definition, characteristics, and underlying causes, we can approach the journey of decluttering our minds and environments with empathy and knowledge.

# CHAPTER 2: RECOGNIZING THE SIGNS AND SYMPTOMS

Recognizing the signs and symptoms of hoarding disorder is crucial in order to identify and address this condition effectively. Hoarding disorder is not simply a matter of being messy or disorganized; it is a complex mental health issue that requires understanding and compassion.

# Understanding Hoarding Disorder

Hoarding disorder is characterized by excessive acquisition and difficulty in discarding possessions. It goes beyond normal clutter or collecting behaviors and significantly impacts a person's daily life. It is important to recognize that hoarding disorder is not a personal choice or a reflection of laziness or selfishness. Rather, it is a psychological condition that requires appropriate intervention and support.

# The Signs of Hoarding Disorder

Hoarding disorder can manifest in various ways, and it is essential to be aware of the signs and symptoms. Some common indications include: 1. Persistent difficulty letting go of possessions: Individuals with hoarding disorder often have an extreme emotional attachment to objects and struggle to discard items, even those with little or no value. 2. Excessive clutter and disorganization: Hoarding disorder leads to a significant accumulation of clutter, which may render parts of the living space unusable or even pose health and safety risks. 3. Strong emotional response to discarding: Discarding possessions may cause distress, anxiety, or intense guilt for individuals with hoarding disorder. They may ruminate over the discarded items or experience a visceral attachment to them. 4. Impaired functioning and distress: Hoarding disorder can severely impact a person's daily life and their relationships. The clutter and disorganization can make it challenging to perform everyday tasks, maintain social connections, or invite others into their homes. 5. Avoidance of decluttering or organizing: Hoarding disorder often leads to avoidance behaviors, such as avoiding decluttering, tidying, or organizing. This avoidance can perpetuate and exacerbate the clutter and disorganization in the living environment.

# The Hidden Nature of Hoarding

Hoarding disorder often remains hidden or undisclosed due to feelings of shame, embarrassment, and fear of judgment. Many individuals with hoarding disorder may go to great lengths to hide their hoarding behaviors, making it difficult for friends, family, and even mental health professionals to recognize and address the problem.

# Seeking Professional Help

Recognizing the signs and symptoms of hoarding disorder is the first step towards seeking professional help. If you or someone you know exhibits these signs, it is essential to consult with a mental health professional who specializes in hoarding disorder. This chapter has provided an overview of the signs and symptoms of hoarding disorder. It is crucial to understand that hoarding disorder is not a personal failing but a complex mental health condition that requires empathy and support. By recognizing the signs and seeking professional help, individuals with hoarding disorder can take steps towards reclaiming their lives and finding a path towards a clutter-free future.

# Chapter 3: Consequences of Hoarding Disorder

Hoarding disorder is not just a harmless habit or a personal preference for clutter. It has serious consequences that can affect various aspects of a person's life. In this chapter, we will explore the significant impact that hoarding disorder can have on individuals, their relationships, and their overall well-being.

## THE EMOTIONAL AND PSYCHOLOGICAL CONSEQUENCES

Living with hoarding disorder can lead to a range of emotional and psychological consequences. People with hoarding disorder often experience intense feelings of anxiety, guilt, shame, and embarrassment about their living conditions and inability to let go of belongings. These negative emotions can significantly impact their self-esteem and overall mental health. The excessive clutter and disorganization in their environment can also cause feelings of overwhelm and helplessness. It becomes increasingly difficult for individuals with hoarding disorder to find items they need or maintain a functional living space. This can lead to frustration, stress, and a sense of being trapped in their own homes. Furthermore, hoarding disorder can isolate individuals from their friends and family. They may feel too embarrassed or ashamed to invite people into their living spaces, leading to social withdrawal and loneliness. This isolation can further exacerbate feelings of depression and anxiety.

# THE PHYSICAL CONSEQUENCES

Hoarding disorder can have physical consequences as well. The excessive clutter can create safety hazards, increasing the risk of falls, fires, and other accidents. Piles of belongings can block pathways and exits, making it challenging to navigate through the home safely. The accumulation of clutter also poses risks to personal hygiene and health. Dust, mold, pests, and other allergens can thrive in hoarded environments, leading to respiratory problems, allergies, and infections. The unsanitary conditions can attract rodents and insects, further increasing the risk of disease transmission. The cluttered living spaces can also impede necessary maintenance and repairs, causing further deterioration of the home and potential structural damage. This can lead to costly expenses and even render the living space unlivable.

# IMPACT ON RELATIONSHIPS

Hoarding disorder not only affects the individual with the condition but can also strain relationships with loved ones. Family members or partners may feel frustrated, overwhelmed, and helpless in trying to address and cope with the clutter. It can lead to tension, arguments, and a breakdown in communication. The hoarding behavior can also cause strain on relationships when it comes to shared living spaces. Other household members may be unable to use common areas, leading to a loss of functionality and a decrease in the quality of life for everyone involved. Additionally, the emotional and psychological consequences experienced by individuals with hoarding disorder can impact their ability to form and maintain healthy relationships. Feelings of shame, embarrassment, and isolation can hinder social interactions and prevent individuals from seeking support and connection.

# FINANCIAL CONSEQUENCES

Hoarding disorder can also have significant financial consequences. The cost of acquiring and maintaining excessive possessions can quickly add up. Individuals with hoarding disorder may spend a substantial amount of money on unnecessary items or duplicates without considering the financial strain it puts on them or their loved ones. The clutter and disorganization can also make it challenging to keep track of bills, important documents, and financial obligations. This can result in missed payments, late fees, and other financial consequences that can further compound the stress and burden of hoarding disorder. In the next chapter, we will delve deeper into the emotional and psychological impact of hoarding disorder. We will explore the various ways it affects the well-being and quality of life of individuals, and discuss strategies for addressing and managing these consequences.

# Chapter 4: The Emotional and Psychological Impact

In hoarding disorder, the accumulation of excessive possessions goes beyond just physical clutter; it also has a significant emotional and psychological impact on individuals. Understanding these impacts is crucial in addressing the root causes of hoarding disorder and finding effective treatment strategies.

## THE EMOTIONAL TOLL

Living in a cluttered and disorganized environment can evoke a range of negative emotions, including anxiety, guilt, shame, embarrassment, overwhelm, helplessness, frustration, stress, and isolation. Individuals with hoarding disorder often feel overwhelmed by their possessions and the inability to manage them properly. The constant presence of clutter can lead to a sense of chaos and make it challenging to find essential items or maintain a functional living space.

## PSYCHOLOGICAL CONSEQUENCES

Hoarding disorder can also have serious psychological consequences. The emotional attachment to possessions is a key characteristic of hoarding, leading individuals to assign high value and significance to even seemingly insignificant or useless items. The fear of discarding these possessions can cause intense distress and anxiety. Additionally, individuals with hoarding disorder may exhibit perfectionist tendencies, fearing that they will make a mistake when deciding what to keep or discard. This fear of making the wrong choice can paralyze them and make the decluttering process incredibly difficult. Furthermore, hoarding disorder can contribute to a sense of identity for some individuals. Possessions may serve as a connection to the past or a representation of one's personal history. Letting go of these possessions may feel like losing a part of oneself, which can lead to a deep emotional struggle.

# THE IMPACT ON RELATIONSHIPS

The emotional and psychological impacts of hoarding disorder can strain relationships with loved ones. Family members may become frustrated, resentful, or concerned about the living conditions and the individual's well-being. Tension, arguments, and a breakdown in communication are common in households affected by hoarding disorder. Moreover, the excessive clutter and disorganization can make it challenging for others to visit or stay in the hoarder's home. This can lead to feelings of isolation and social withdrawal, further exacerbating the emotional toll on the individual.

# SEEKING SUPPORT

It is crucial for individuals with hoarding disorder to seek support and understanding from mental health professionals, support groups, and loved ones. Therapy can help individuals explore the emotional and psychological factors contributing to their hoarding behavior and develop coping mechanisms to address them. By seeking professional help, individuals can begin to heal emotionally and improve their overall well-being.

# CONCLUSION

The emotional and psychological impact of hoarding disorder is significant and cannot be taken lightly. It is essential to approach hoarding disorder with compassion and understanding, recognizing that it is not a personal choice or a reflection of laziness or selfishness. By addressing the emotional toll and seeking appropriate treatment, individuals can begin the journey towards decluttering their minds and achieving a sense of peace and order in their lives.

# Chapter 5: Getting to the Root Cause

Understanding the root cause of hoarding disorder is essential in developing effective strategies for managing and overcoming the condition. Hoarding is a complex issue that arises from a combination of genetic, environmental, and psychological factors. Identifying and addressing the underlying causes can help individuals gain insight into their hoarding behaviors and promote long-lasting change.

## EXPLORING GENETIC FACTORS

Research suggests that genetics play a role in hoarding disorder. Studies have found that individuals with first-degree relatives who hoard are more likely to develop the condition themselves. Certain genes may be associated with difficulties in regulating emotions and decision-making processes, which can contribute to hoarding tendencies. While genetics can increase the risk of developing hoarding disorder, they do not determine an individual's destiny. Understanding the genetic component of hoarding disorder can offer insights into potential vulnerabilities, but it is crucial to remember that environment and psychological factors also play significant roles.

# EXAMINING ENVIRONMENTAL INFLUENCES

The physical environment in which a person grows up or lives can contribute to the development of hoarding disorder. Certain factors, such as childhood experiences or exposure to trauma, can trigger hoarding behaviors as a way to cope with emotional distress. Individuals who grew up in cluttered or chaotic households may replicate these environments as adults. Additionally, societal and cultural influences can impact the development of hoarding disorder. Living in a consumer-driven society that values material possessions can fuel excessive acquiring and difficulty discarding. Media, advertising, and societal norms that prioritize material wealth and accumulation can contribute to the emergence of hoarding behaviors.

# UNDERSTANDING PSYCHOLOGICAL FACTORS

Psychological factors, such as underlying mental health conditions, can significantly contribute to hoarding disorder. Many individuals with hoarding tendencies also experience anxiety, depression, obsessive-compulsive disorder (OCD), attention-deficit/hyperactivity disorder (ADHD), or other mental health conditions. Hoarding behaviors may serve as coping mechanisms to alleviate distress or fill emotional voids. Trauma and past experiences can also shape hoarding behaviors. Possessions can provide a sense of security, comfort, and control for individuals who have experienced loss, abandonment, or significant life changes. The accumulation of possessions may be an attempt to fill emotional voids or maintain a connection to the past.

## SEEKING PROFESSIONAL HELP

Getting to the root cause of hoarding disorder often requires the guidance of mental health professionals. Therapists and psychologists specializing in hoarding disorder can help individuals explore the underlying causes of their behaviors and develop coping strategies to address emotional distress. Therapy sessions may involve talking through past experiences, examining thought patterns and beliefs, and identifying triggers for hoarding behaviors. By understanding the root cause, individuals can gain insight and develop healthier ways of coping with emotions, stress, and trauma.

# CULTIVATING SELF-REFLECTION

In addition to professional help, self-reflection plays a crucial role in understanding the root causes of hoarding disorder. Taking time to reflect on personal experiences, emotions, and thought patterns can provide valuable insights into the origins of hoarding behaviors. Journaling, mindfulness practices, and engaging in self-care activities can facilitate self-reflection. It is essential to approach this process with self-compassion and patience, as it may bring up challenging emotions. Creating a safe and supportive environment for self-reflection can contribute to personal growth and the development of healthier coping mechanisms. Understanding the root causes of hoarding disorder is an ongoing and dynamic process. It requires a combination of self-exploration, professional guidance, and a commitment to personal growth. By delving into these underlying factors, individuals can gain a deeper understanding of their hoarding behaviors and work toward establishing a clutter-free and balanced life.

# Chapter 6: Building Motivation for Change

Change can be a difficult process, especially when it comes to hoarding disorder. The accumulation of possessions and the attachment to them can make it challenging to even consider decluttering and organizing. However, building motivation for change is an essential step towards overcoming hoarding disorder and reclaiming a clutter-free life.

## THE IMPORTANCE OF MOTIVATION

Motivation is the driving force behind any successful change. It is what propels individuals to take action and make the necessary steps towards a desired goal. In the case of hoarding disorder, building motivation is crucial because it provides the necessary push to address the underlying issues and begin the process of decluttering.

# UNDERSTANDING MOTIVATIONAL FACTORS

Motivational factors vary from person to person, and it's important to recognize what specifically drives each individual towards change. Here are some common motivational factors that can help build the momentum needed for decluttering:

## Improved Quality of Life

Many individuals with hoarding disorder experience a diminished quality of life due to the clutter and disorganization in their physical environment. Building motivation by envisioning a clutter-free and organized space can encourage individuals to make the necessary changes to improve their living conditions.

## Health and Safety Concerns

Hoarding disorder can pose significant health and safety risks. Excessive clutter can lead to fire hazards, hinder mobility, and create unsanitary living conditions. Motivation can come from recognizing the potential dangers and wanting to create a safe and healthy living environment.

## Positive Relationships

Hoarding disorder can strain relationships with loved ones, leading to isolation and a breakdown in communication. Building motivation by considering the positive impact that decluttering can have on relationships can be a powerful driving force for change.

## Financial Freedom

The financial consequences of hoarding disorder can be overwhelming. Excessive spending on unnecessary items and the cost of maintaining a cluttered environment can cause financial strain. Motivation can stem from the desire to regain control over finances and experience the freedom that comes with living a clutter-free life.

## STRATEGIES TO BUILD MOTIVATION

While building motivation can be challenging, there are strategies that can help individuals with hoarding disorder kick-start their journey towards change:

# Visualize the Desired Outcome

Encourage individuals to imagine what their ideal living space would look like. Visualizing a clutter-free and organized environment can create a sense of excitement and motivation.

# Set Realistic Goals

Breaking down the decluttering process into smaller, achievable goals can make it more manageable and less overwhelming. Celebrating each victory along the way can further enhance motivation.

# Stay Connected to the Why

Remind individuals of their primary motivation for change. Continuously reinforcing the benefits of a clutter-free life can help maintain motivation during challenging times.

# Seek Support

Support from loved ones, support groups, or professional therapists can be invaluable in building and sustaining motivation. Surrounding oneself with understanding and supportive individuals can help boost morale and provide encouragement throughout the journey.

## CONCLUSION

Building motivation for change is a crucial step in the process of overcoming hoarding disorder. Recognizing the importance of motivation, understanding personal motivational factors, and implementing strategies to build and sustain motivation can help individuals embark on their journey towards a clutter-free and organized life. Remember, change is possible, and with the right mindset and support, individuals can break free from the grip of hoarding disorder and embrace a happier, more fulfilling life.

# Chapter 7: Acceptance and Commitment Therapy

Acceptance and Commitment Therapy (ACT) is an evidence-based therapeutic approach that can be beneficial for individuals struggling with hoarding disorder. This chapter will explore how ACT can help individuals with hoarding disorder develop acceptance, mindfulness, and commit to actions that align with their values.

# UNDERSTANDING ACCEPTANCE AND COMMITMENT THERAPY

Acceptance and Commitment Therapy is based on the principle that suffering is a normal part of the human experience, and attempts to control or avoid suffering can often lead to more distress. Instead, ACT focuses on accepting difficult thoughts and emotions while committing to actions that are meaningful and consistent with one's values. In the context of hoarding disorder, ACT can help individuals develop acceptance and non-judgmental awareness of their hoarding thoughts and emotions. It helps them understand that these thoughts and emotions are not who they are, but simply internal experiences that they can observe. This shift in perspective can be powerful in reducing the emotional distress associated with hoarding.

# DEVELOPING ACCEPTANCE AND MINDFULNESS

One of the primary goals of ACT is to develop acceptance and mindfulness skills. Acceptance involves acknowledging and allowing difficult thoughts, emotions, and sensations to arise without trying to push them away or change them. This allows individuals to develop a more helpful relationship with their hoarding thoughts and emotions. Mindfulness, on the other hand, involves actively paying attention to the present moment with curiosity and non-judgment. By practicing mindfulness, individuals can observe their hoarding thoughts and emotions without getting caught up in them. This allows them to respond to these thoughts and emotions in a more skillful and intentional manner.

# IDENTIFYING VALUES AND TAKING COMMITTED ACTION

Another important aspect of Acceptance and Commitment Therapy is helping individuals clarify their values and take committed action towards them. Values are what give our lives meaning and purpose. In the context of hoarding disorder, values may include having a clean and organized living space, maintaining healthy relationships, and living a fulfilling life. Once individuals have identified their values, ACT helps them align their actions with these values. This can involve setting small, achievable goals that are in line with their values and taking steps towards decluttering and organizing their physical environment. By committing to these actions, individuals can make progress towards creating a clutter-free and fulfilling life.

# WORKING WITH A THERAPIST

Acceptance and Commitment Therapy is typically conducted with the guidance of a trained therapist. A therapist can provide support and guidance in developing acceptance, mindfulness, and aligning actions with values. They can also help individuals identify unhelpful patterns of thinking and behavior related to hoarding and work towards changing them.

# THE BENEFITS OF ACCEPTANCE AND COMMITMENT THERAPY

Acceptance and Commitment Therapy has been shown to be effective in reducing distress and improving overall well-being for individuals with hoarding disorder. By developing acceptance, mindfulness, and aligning actions with values, individuals can cultivate a healthier relationship with their hoarding thoughts and emotions. ACT can also help individuals develop essential skills for maintaining progress and preventing relapse. By practicing acceptance and mindfulness, individuals can continue to respond to hoarding thoughts and emotions in a more skillful and intentional manner. In conclusion, Acceptance and Commitment Therapy offers a valuable approach to healing and recovery for individuals with hoarding disorder. By developing acceptance, mindfulness, and aligning actions with values, individuals can navigate their hoarding thoughts and emotions more effectively and move towards a clutter-free and fulfilling life. Seek out the guidance of a trained therapist to explore this therapeutic approach further.

# Chapter 8: Cognitive-Behavioral Therapy

Cognitive-Behavioral Therapy (CBT) is a widely recognized and effective treatment approach for hoarding disorder. It focuses on identifying and modifying unhelpful thoughts and behaviors that contribute to hoarding behaviors. CBT is a goal-oriented and structured therapy that helps individuals develop practical strategies to overcome hoarding. One of the key principles of CBT is that our thoughts, feelings, and actions are interconnected. In the context of hoarding disorder, individuals may have distorted beliefs and thoughts about their possessions, such as "I might need it someday" or "This item has sentimental value." These thoughts can drive the compulsion to acquire and the difficulty in discarding items. CBT aims to challenge and replace these unhelpful thoughts with more realistic and rational ones. The therapist works collaboratively with the individual to identify and examine the thoughts and beliefs that contribute to the hoarding behaviors. By exploring the evidence for and against these thoughts, individuals can begin to develop a more balanced perspective on their possessions. In addition to cognitive restructuring, CBT also involves behavioral interventions. These interventions focus on gradually exposing individuals to the anxiety-provoking situations related to discarding possessions. This exposure helps individuals build tolerance to the discomfort associated with discarding and reduces the fear response. During the therapy sessions, individuals with hoarding disorder may also learn specific skills to enhance their decision-making abilities. This includes categorizing possessions, organizing techniques, and developing strategies for maintaining a clutter-free environment. The therapist may provide practical guidance and support to help individuals implement these skills in their daily lives. CBT for hoarding disorder typically involves regular sessions with a trained therapist over a specified period of time. The duration and frequency of therapy may vary depending on the individual's needs. It is important to work with a therapist who has experience and expertise in treating hoarding disorder to ensure the best possible outcomes. In addition to formal therapy sessions, individuals can practice CBT techniques on their own. This may involve keeping a thought diary to track unhelpful thoughts and challenging them using evidence-based reasoning. Other strategies, such as setting specific goals, using distraction techniques, and seeking social support, can also support the CBT process. Overall, CBT provides individuals with hoarding disorder the tools and skills necessary to challenge their thoughts, modify their behaviors, and create lasting change. It empowers individuals to take control of their possessions and create a clutter-free and more functional living space. Remember, overcoming hoarding disorder is a journey, and CBT is just one part of that journey. It is essential to approach the process with patience, self-compassion, and support from loved ones and professionals. With dedication and the right therapeutic approach, individuals can overcome hoarding disorder and create a more organized and fulfilling life.

# Chapter 9: Dialectical Behavior Therapy

Dialectical Behavior Therapy (DBT) is a specialized form of therapy that has shown effectiveness in treating hoarding disorder. Developed by psychologist Marsha Linehan, DBT was initially designed to address borderline personality disorder but has since been adapted for various mental health conditions, including hoarding disorder. DBT is based on the concept of dialectics, which recognizes that conflicting thoughts and emotions can both be valid and true. It integrates acceptance and change-oriented strategies to help individuals develop skills for emotional regulation, distress tolerance, interpersonal effectiveness, and mindfulness. Here are some key components and strategies of DBT that can be helpful for individuals with hoarding disorder:

# 1. MINDFULNESS

Mindfulness is a fundamental aspect of DBT and involves cultivating non-judgmental awareness of the present moment. By practicing mindfulness, individuals with hoarding disorder can develop greater insight into their thoughts, emotions, and the underlying reasons behind their hoarding behaviors. Mindfulness can also help increase self-compassion and reduce the judgment and shame often associated with hoarding.

# 2. EMOTIONAL REGULATION

Hoarding disorder is often accompanied by intense emotions such as anxiety, sadness, and fear. DBT aims to help individuals regulate these emotions by teaching skills for identifying and labeling emotions, understanding emotional triggers, and finding healthy ways to cope with emotional distress. By developing healthier emotional regulation strategies, individuals with hoarding disorder can reduce the reliance on excessive acquiring and clutter as a means of emotional comfort.

# 3. DISTRESS TOLERANCE

Hoarding disorder can be associated with high levels of distress and discomfort when faced with decisions about discarding possessions or organizing spaces. DBT helps individuals build distress tolerance skills, enabling them to face and tolerate distressing situations without resorting to hoarding behaviors. Techniques such as self-soothing, distraction, and radical acceptance can be helpful in managing distress and preventing impulsive acquiring or excessive cluttering.

# 4. INTERPERSONAL EFFECTIVENESS

Hoarding disorder can strain relationships with loved ones and make it challenging to engage in healthy communication and assertiveness. DBT helps individuals develop skills for effective interpersonal interactions, including setting boundaries, expressing needs and wants, and resolving conflicts. By improving interpersonal skills, individuals with hoarding disorder can strengthen relationships and decrease feelings of isolation and shame.

# 5. DIALECTICAL STRATEGIES

DBT emphasizes the integration of opposing viewpoints and finding a middle ground. This dialectical approach can be used to challenge black-and-white thinking often associated with hoarding disorder. By exploring and challenging rigid thoughts and beliefs about possessions, individuals with hoarding disorder can develop a more balanced and flexible mindset which supports decluttering and organization. DBT is typically conducted through individual therapy sessions, group therapy, and skills training. It is important for individuals with hoarding disorder to work with a therapist trained in DBT techniques to ensure a personalized and effective treatment plan. In conclusion, Dialectical Behavior Therapy (DBT) offers valuable strategies and techniques for individuals with hoarding disorder. By addressing emotional regulation, distress tolerance, mindfulness, interpersonal effectiveness, and dialectical thinking, DBT can promote positive changes and support the transition from hoarding to a clutter-free life.

# Chapter 10: Mindfulness Techniques

Life is filled with distractions and it's easy to get caught up in the chaos of our surroundings. For individuals with hoarding disorder, the cluttered environment can further contribute to feelings of overwhelm and anxiety. However, incorporating mindfulness techniques into daily life can be a powerful tool for managing these challenges and ultimately leading to a clutter-free mind and environment.

## WHAT IS MINDFULNESS?

Mindfulness is the practice of intentionally paying attention to the present moment, without judgment. Instead of being carried away by thoughts of the past or future, mindfulness allows us to fully immerse ourselves in the here and now. This practice can help individuals with hoarding disorder develop a greater sense of self-awareness and make conscious choices about their thoughts, behaviors, and environment.

# THE BENEFITS OF MINDFULNESS FOR HOARDING DISORDER

Mindfulness has been shown to have numerous benefits for individuals with hoarding disorder. By cultivating mindfulness, individuals can:

## 1. Improve Emotional Regulation:

Mindfulness helps individuals observe their emotions without becoming overwhelmed by them. By developing a non-judgmental stance towards their emotions, individuals can learn to accept and regulate their emotional responses to the challenges of hoarding disorder.

## 2. Reduce Impulsive Acquiring:

Mindfulness allows individuals to pause and reflect before making impulsive decisions about acquiring new possessions. By bringing awareness to their desires and motivations, individuals can make more intentional choices about what they truly need and value.

# 3. Increase Clarity and Decision-Making:

The practice of mindfulness enhances cognitive abilities and helps individuals break free from the cognitive rigidity often associated with hoarding disorder. By cultivating a clear and focused mind, individuals can approach decision-making with greater clarity and confidence.

# 4. Reduce Anxiety and Distress:

Mindfulness can help individuals manage anxiety and distress associated with hoarding disorder. By focusing on the present moment and non-judgmentally observing their thoughts and feelings, individuals can decrease the intensity of their anxiety and find a sense of calm amidst the chaos.

# 5. Enhance Self-Compassion:

Mindfulness encourages individuals to treat themselves with kindness and compassion. By observing their self-critical thoughts without judgment, individuals can learn to be more forgiving and understanding towards themselves. This self-compassion can have a positive impact on their well-being and motivation to make changes.

# INCORPORATING MINDFULNESS INTO DAILY LIFE

There are several mindfulness techniques that individuals with hoarding disorder can incorporate into their daily lives to cultivate a clutter-free mind and environment:

## 1. Mindful Breathing:

Take a few minutes each day to focus on your breath. Close your eyes and bring attention to your breath as it enters and leaves your body. Notice the sensation of the breath and let go of any distracting thoughts. Engaging in mindful breathing can help you calm your mind and bring clarity to your thoughts.

## 2. Body Scan Meditation:

Engage in a body scan meditation to bring awareness to your physical sensations. Start from the top of your head and slowly move down your body, noticing any tension, discomfort, or areas of relaxation. By connecting with your body, you can become more attuned to your needs and better understand the impact of clutter on your physical well-being.

# 3. Mindful Eating:

Take the time to savor each bite of your meals. Pay attention to the colors, textures, and flavors of the food. Eating mindfully allows you to fully experience the nourishment and pleasure of your meals, reducing the need for emotional comfort through acquiring possessions.

# 4. Mindful Walking:

Engage in mindful walking by focusing on the sensations of each step. Notice the feeling of your feet touching the ground, the movement of your body, and the sounds and sights around you. This practice can help ground you in the present moment and reduce distractions from acquiring behaviors.

# 5. Mindful Decluttering:

When engaging in decluttering activities, practice mindfulness by bringing your full attention to the task at hand. Notice the physical sensations as you pick up each item, observe any emotional attachments or resistance that arise, and make intentional decisions about what to keep and what to let go of.

# THE POWER OF MINDFULNESS IN HOARDING RECOVERY

Mindfulness is a powerful tool for individuals with hoarding disorder to cultivate self-awareness, regulate emotions, and make intentional choices. By incorporating mindfulness techniques into daily life, individuals can create a space for clarity, compassion, and ultimately, a clutter-free mind and environment. Remember, mindfulness is a practice that requires patience and commitment. Start with small moments of mindfulness throughout your day and gradually expand the practice. Over time, you'll experience the transformational power of mindfulness in your journey towards overcoming hoarding disorder and embracing a clutter-free life.

# Chapter 11: Decluttering Your Physical Environment

The physical environment plays a significant role in hoarding disorder. It is essential to address the clutter and disorganization to create a calm and functional space. Decluttering your physical environment is a crucial step towards overcoming hoarding disorder and improving your overall well-being.

## UNDERSTANDING THE IMPACT OF CLUTTER

Living in a cluttered environment can be overwhelming and affect various aspects of your life. Clutter not only takes up physical space but also occupies mental and emotional space. It can evoke feelings of anxiety, stress, and even contribute to depression. The disorganization can also make it difficult to find important items when you need them, causing further frustration and wasting time.

# GETTING STARTED WITH DECLUTTERING

Decluttering can feel like an overwhelming task, but it is essential to break it down into manageable steps. Here are some strategies to help you get started:

## 1. Set Realistic Goals

Start small and set achievable goals. It is better to declutter one area at a time rather than trying to tackle the entire space in one go. By setting small goals, you can maintain motivation and see progress along the way.

## 2. Sort and Categorize

As you begin decluttering, sort your belongings into categories. This process allows you to evaluate each item and make decisions about what to keep, donate, or discard. Categorizing items can also make it easier to find specific things in the future.

# 3. Letting Go of Sentimental Items

One of the most challenging aspects of decluttering is letting go of sentimental items. It can be challenging to part with belongings that hold memories or emotional attachments. However, it is essential to prioritize your well-being and make decisions based on what is truly valuable to you in the present moment.

# 4. Seek Support

Decluttering can be an emotionally challenging process. It can be helpful to seek support from a trusted friend, family member, or professional organizer. They can provide encouragement, guidance, and a fresh perspective.

# ORGANIZING SYSTEMS AND STRATEGIES

Once you have decluttered your physical environment, it is crucial to establish organizing systems and strategies to maintain order. Here are some tips:

# 1. Designate Specific Spaces

Assign specific spaces for different categories of items. For example, create designated areas for books, clothing, kitchen utensils, and so on. This will make it easier to find and put away items in the future.

# 2. Use Storage Solutions

Invest in practical storage solutions such as shelves, bins, and drawer organizers. These tools can help maximize space and keep your belongings organized. Remember to label containers to make it easier to find items later.

# 3. Establish Routines

Consistency is key when it comes to maintaining an organized space. Establish daily or weekly routines for tidying and putting things away. This can help prevent clutter from building up over time.

# 4. Regular Maintenance

Regular maintenance is critical to prevent clutter from returning. Schedule regular decluttering sessions to reassess your belongings and ensure everything has its place. This habit will help you stay organized and prevent a build-up of clutter in the future.

# BENEFITS OF A DECLUTTERED SPACE

Decluttering your physical environment offers numerous benefits, including: - Reduced stress and anxiety: A clutter-free space can create a sense of calm and promote relaxation. - Improved productivity: An organized environment allows you to focus and be more efficient in your daily tasks. - Enhanced mental well-being: Living in a clean and organized space can positively impact your mental health, reducing feelings of overwhelm and improving overall happiness. - Better physical health: Decluttering can reduce allergens and create a healthier living environment, decreasing the risk of respiratory issues and allergies. Remember that decluttering is a process, and it takes time. Be patient with yourself and celebrate each small step towards a clutter-free space. The goal is to create an environment that supports your well-being and allows you to live a fulfilling life. Keep up the momentum, and you'll soon embrace the benefits of a decluttered physical environment.

# Chapter 12: Sorting and Categorizing Belongings

Sorting and categorizing belongings is a crucial step in the decluttering process for individuals with hoarding disorder. It involves creating a clear and organized system for managing possessions, making it easier to navigate and maintain an orderly living space. In this chapter, we will explore effective strategies for sorting and categorizing belongings to help individuals with hoarding disorder overcome the challenges of excessive clutter and disorganization.

## THE IMPORTANCE OF SORTING AND CATEGORIZING

When faced with a cluttered environment, it can be overwhelming to know where to begin. Sorting and categorizing belongings provide a structured approach to organizing possessions and creating a sense of control over one's living space. By assigning categories to different items, individuals can easily locate and access what they need while reducing the feeling of being surrounded by chaos. Sorting and categorizing also help individuals assess the value and significance of their belongings. It allows them to prioritize what truly matters, making it easier to let go of items that no longer serve a purpose or hold sentimental value. By establishing clear categories, individuals can make informed decisions about what to keep, donate, or discard.

# STRATEGIES FOR EFFECTIVE SORTING AND CATEGORIZING

1. **Start Small:** Begin the sorting and categorizing process in a manageable area, such as a single drawer or shelf. Breaking down the task into smaller, more achievable steps can prevent overwhelm and maintain motivation. 2. **Create Categories:** Establish different categories based on the type of items you have. Common categories include clothing, books, electronics, sentimental items, and household supplies. It is essential to tailor the categories to your specific belongings and needs. 3. **Sorting Criteria:** Develop criteria for deciding which category an item belongs to. Consider factors such as functionality, frequency of use, sentimental value, and condition. This strategy helps create a consistent and objective approach to sorting. 4. **One at a Time:** Focus on sorting and categorizing one item at a time. Avoid getting distracted by other items or jumping

between categories. By staying focused on one item, you can make quicker decisions and maintain clarity. 5. **Stay Mindful:** Practice mindfulness during the sorting process. Be present and aware of your thoughts and emotions as you handle each item. Use this opportunity to reflect on any attachments or emotional ties you may have to certain possessions. 6. **Stay Organized:** Use containers, bins, and labels to keep items within each category together. This not only makes it easier to locate specific items later but also helps maintain order and prevents future clutter. 7. **Ask for Help:** Don't hesitate to ask for assistance from friends, family, or professionals. Having a second opinion or someone to provide support can make the sorting process more efficient and less overwhelming. 8. **Set Realistic Goals:** Break down the sorting and categorizing process into manageable chunks and set achievable goals. Celebrate your progress along the way, even if it's just sorting a small pile of items. Remember, every step forward counts.

# MAINTAINING ORDER AND EVALUATING PROGRESS

After sorting and categorizing belongings, it is essential to maintain order and regularly evaluate your progress. Here are some strategies to help you stay organized and track your achievements:

1. **Regular Cleaning Sessions:** Schedule regular cleaning sessions to declutter and reorganize your space. Set aside a specific day or time each week or month for this purpose. 2. **Review Categories:** Periodically review and refine your categories. As you become more familiar with your belongings and your organizing needs change, adjusting the categories can improve efficiency and effectiveness. 3. **Adopt a "One In, One Out" Rule:** To prevent new clutter from accumulating, establish a rule that for every new item you bring into your home, you must donate or discard an existing item. This practice helps maintain a balanced and clutter-free space. 4. **Keep a Progress Journal:** Maintain a journal where you can track your progress. Document the areas you have successfully sorted and the challenges you have overcome. This journal can serve as a source of motivation and a reminder of how far you have come. 5. **Celebrate Achievements:** Acknowledge and celebrate your achievements as you make progress in organizing your belongings. Treat yourself to a small reward or engage in a pleasurable activity to reinforce positive behavior and maintain motivation. Remember, sorting and categorizing belongings is not a one-time task. It requires ongoing maintenance to prevent clutter

from reaccumulating. With dedication and perseverance, the process of sorting and categorizing can bring a sense of order and peace to your living environment, helping you on your journey to a clutter-free life. Next, we will explore effective strategies for organizing systems and strategies to further enhance the functionality and orderliness of your living space.

# Chapter 13: Organizing Systems and Strategies

Organizing systems and strategies are essential for maintaining order and creating a clutter-free environment. Once you have sorted and categorized your belongings, it's time to establish a system that will help you stay organized and prevent future clutter from accumulating. In this chapter, we will explore various organizing systems and strategies that can be tailored to your specific needs.

## THE IMPORTANCE OF ORGANIZATION

Having a well-organized space not only promotes a sense of calm and harmony but also increases efficiency and productivity. When everything has a designated place, it becomes easier to find what you need and eliminates the frustration of rummaging through clutter. Additionally, an organized environment can improve mental well-being and reduce stress levels, allowing you to focus on the things that truly matter.

# DESIGNATING SPECIFIC SPACES

One effective organizing strategy is to designate specific spaces for different categories of belongings. This means assigning a dedicated area for each type of item, whether it's clothing, books, kitchenware, or sentimental items. When everything has its own place, it becomes easier to maintain order and prevents items from getting mixed up or misplaced. Consider using labels or color-coded storage containers to clearly identify where each item belongs. This will not only make it easier for you to find things but also for others who may need to access your belongings. Remember to update the designated spaces as your inventory of possessions changes, ensuring that everything has a designated spot.

# USING STORAGE SOLUTIONS

Storage solutions play a crucial role in keeping your belongings organized and easily accessible. Here are a few ideas for effective storage solutions: 1. Shelving units: Install sturdy shelving units in your home to maximize vertical space and provide additional storage options for items that are not frequently used. 2. Bins and baskets: Utilize plastic or woven bins and baskets to group similar items together. These can be placed on shelves, under beds, or in closets to keep items organized and out of sight. 3. Drawer dividers: Use dividers or small trays within drawers to create separate compartments for different items. This makes it easier to locate specific items and prevents them from getting mixed together. 4. Hanging organizers: Hang organizers on the back of doors or in closets to store items such as shoes, scarves, or accessories. This maximizes space and keeps items easily visible and accessible. 5. Clear containers: Opt for clear containers to store items like craft supplies, office supplies, or small accessories. Being able to see what's inside the containers eliminates the need to rummage through boxes or bins.

# ESTABLISHING ROUTINES AND REGULAR MAINTENANCE

Once you have implemented an organizing system and utilized storage solutions, it is crucial to establish routines and regular maintenance habits to sustain a clutter-free environment. Here are some strategies to consider: 1. Daily tidying: Set aside a few minutes each day to do a quick tidying session. Put away items that have been left out, discard any trash or unwanted items, and ensure everything is in its designated place. 2. Weekly decluttering: Schedule a regular time each week to go through different areas of your home and declutter any items that may have accumulated. This will help you maintain a clutter-free space and prevent things from piling up again. 3. Don't procrastinate: When you notice something is out of place or no longer serves a purpose, address it immediately. Avoid the temptation to set it aside for later, as this can lead to the reoccurrence of clutter. 4. Practice the "one in, one out" rule: For every new item you bring into your home, make a point to remove one similar item. This ensures that your space doesn't become overwhelmed with unnecessary belongings.

# CELEBRATING SMALL WINS

Decluttering and organizing your space is a journey that takes time and effort. It's important to acknowledge and celebrate the small wins along the way. When you successfully organize a specific area or complete a decluttering task, take a moment to appreciate your accomplishments. Reward yourself with something you enjoy, such as a favorite treat or a relaxing activity. Celebrating these small wins will help keep you motivated and make the process more enjoyable.

# CONCLUSION

Implementing effective organizing systems and strategies is crucial for maintaining a clutter-free environment. Designating specific spaces, utilizing storage solutions, establishing routines, and practicing regular maintenance are key components of an organized lifestyle. Remember to celebrate your progress along the way and embrace the benefits of a well-organized space – increased efficiency, reduced stress, and improved overall well-being.

# Chapter 14: Establishing Routines and Maintenance

Creating and maintaining a clutter-free environment is not a one-time task but an ongoing commitment. In this chapter, we will explore the importance of establishing routines and maintenance strategies to ensure long-term success in managing hoarding disorder.

## THE IMPORTANCE OF ROUTINES

Routines play a crucial role in maintaining order and preventing the re-accumulation of clutter. By incorporating regular habits into your daily life, you can keep your environment organized and prevent the chaos of hoarding from reoccurring. One of the key benefits of establishing routines is that they create a sense of stability and predictability in your life. When you have set times and activities dedicated to decluttering, organizing, and cleaning, it becomes easier to stay on top of these tasks and prevent them from becoming overwhelming. Routines also help to build discipline and consistency. By committing to daily or weekly tasks, such as sorting through items, tidying up, or deep cleaning certain areas, you develop a habit of maintaining your clutter-free environment. Over time, these routines will become more ingrained, making it easier to stick to them and avoid falling back into old hoarding patterns.

# CREATING A MAINTENANCE PLAN

To establish effective routines, it is important to create a maintenance plan tailored to your specific needs. Here are some steps to help you develop a plan:

# 1. Assess Your Environment

Take a look at your living space and identify areas that require regular attention. This may include designated clutter-prone spots, high-traffic areas, or storage spaces that tend to become disorganized quickly. By understanding which areas need the most attention, you can prioritize your maintenance efforts.

# 2. Break Tasks into Manageable Chunks

Clutter can feel overwhelming, but by breaking down maintenance tasks into smaller, manageable chunks, you can make the process more attainable. For example, instead of dedicating an entire day to cleaning, allocate specific time slots or days for different tasks like decluttering, organizing, and cleaning. This will prevent you from feeling exhausted or discouraged.

# 3. Set Realistic Goals

When establishing routines and maintenance plans, it is essential to set realistic goals. Consider your schedule, energy levels, and other commitments to determine a reasonable amount of time and effort you can dedicate to maintaining your clutter-free environment. Setting achievable goals will help you stay motivated and avoid feeling overwhelmed.

# 4. Create a Schedule

Develop a schedule that incorporates your maintenance tasks into your daily or weekly routine. Block out specific time slots for different activities, such as decluttering a specific room on a designated day, organizing items every evening, or doing a thorough cleaning once a month. Having a set schedule will make it easier to follow through and establish consistency.

# 5. Utilize Reminders and Checklists

To stay on track with your maintenance plan, utilize reminders and checklists. Set alarms or create calendar events to prompt you to complete specific tasks. Create checklists to keep track of what needs to be done and mark off completed tasks. These tools can help you stay organized and ensure you don't overlook any important maintenance activities.

## MAINTAINING MOTIVATION

Establishing routines and sticking to a maintenance plan can sometimes be challenging, especially during periods of stress or when faced with setbacks. Here are some strategies to help you maintain motivation:

# 1. Visualize Your Ideal Living Space

Take a moment to imagine what your clutter-free and organized living space will look like. Visualize the sense of calm and peace that comes with a tidy environment. Keep this mental image in mind as you go through your maintenance tasks, and let it motivate you to stay committed to your routines.

# 2. Celebrate Small Wins

Recognize and celebrate your progress, no matter how small. Each completed maintenance task, no matter how seemingly insignificant, is a step forward in your journey towards a clutter-free life. Reward yourself for your efforts, whether it's with a treat, a break, or engaging in an activity you enjoy.

# 3. Seek Support

Reach out to your support network for encouragement and accountability. Share your maintenance plan with trusted friends or family members who can check in on your progress and offer assistance when needed. Engaging with support groups or online communities can also provide a sense of camaraderie and motivation.

# 4. Reflect on How Far You've Come

Take time to reflect on the progress you have made in your decluttering journey. Remind yourself of the challenges you have overcome and the positive changes you have experienced. Reflecting on your accomplishments can reignite your motivation and inspire you to continue moving forward.

# 5. Be Kind to Yourself

Remember to be kind and patient with yourself throughout the maintenance process. Hoarding disorder is a complex condition, and setbacks may occur. Instead of dwelling on setbacks or mistakes, practice self-compassion and focus on learning from the experience. Treat yourself with the same understanding and forgiveness you would give to a loved one going through a similar journey. By establishing routines and committing to regular maintenance, you can maintain a clutter-free and organized living space. Remember, it is a gradual process, and each small step you take brings you closer to a clutter-free life. Stay consistent, stay motivated, and embrace the peace and serenity that comes with an organized environment.

# Chapter 15: Letting Go of Sentimental Items

## THE EMOTIONAL ATTACHMENT TO SENTIMENTAL ITEMS

Letting go of sentimental items can be one of the most challenging aspects of decluttering for individuals with hoarding disorder. These items hold deep emotional value and serve as a connection to cherished memories, people, or significant life events. The attachment to these items can make it incredibly difficult to consider parting with them.

## Understanding the Reasons for Emotional Attachments

To effectively address the hoarding behavior, it is essential to explore and understand the reasons behind the emotional attachments. Sentimental items often represent a sense of identity, nostalgia, or a feeling of comfort and security. They may serve as reminders of happier times or loved ones who are no longer present. Acknowledging the emotional significance of these items is the first step towards loosening the grip they have on one's life. It's important to recognize that the memories associated with these items reside within oneself and not solely within the physical objects.

## Shifting Perspectives on Sentimental Items

Changing perspectives on sentimental items can help individuals with hoarding disorder develop a healthier relationship with their belongings. It involves challenging the assumptions about what these items mean and exploring alternative ways to preserve memories and honor the past. One approach is to separate the item itself from the memories it represents. Recognizing that the memories and emotions are independent of the physical object allows individuals to consider alternative methods for preserving the sentimental value.

# Strategies for Letting Go

Letting go of sentimental items is a gradual and personal process. Here are some strategies that can be helpful: 1. Reflect on the true significance: Take time to reflect on the true emotional value of each item. Ask yourself if it genuinely brings joy or serves a meaningful purpose in your current life. 2. Prioritize: Set priorities by identifying the items that hold the most significance to you. Focus on keeping a few key items that truly represent your memories and experiences. 3. Create a memory box: If you find it challenging to part with sentimental items altogether, consider creating a memory box. This box can hold a curated selection of items that you treasure the most. Keep in mind that the goal is to limit the number of items and create space for new memories. 4. Digitalize memories: Embrace modern technology and consider digitizing sentimental items, such as photographs, letters, or documents. By scanning or photographing these items, you can preserve the memories without cluttering your physical space. Additionally, digitalization allows for easy access and sharing with loved ones. 5. Seek support: Enlist the help of a trusted friend or family member to provide guidance and support during the decluttering process. Sometimes, having an objective perspective can help you make more rational decisions about what to keep and what to let go. 6. Practice gradual release: If parting with certain items feels too overwhelming, consider a gradual release approach. Start by removing a few items at a time and gradually increase the number as you become more comfortable with letting go. 7. Letting go ceremony: Create a meaningful ritual or ceremony to honor the act of letting go. This could include writing a letter to the object, expressing gratitude for the memories it represents before releasing it.

# Embracing the Freedom of Letting Go

While it can be emotionally challenging, letting go of sentimental items can be liberating. It opens up physical space and fosters a sense of mental and emotional freedom. By decluttering and letting go of the excess, individuals with hoarding disorder can create a more organized and peaceful living environment. Remember, the process of letting go is personal and unique to each individual. It requires patience, compassion, and self-reflection. With time and practice, it is possible to develop healthier attachments to sentimental items and find joy in the memories rather than the physical possessions.

# Chapter 16: Handling Paperwork and Documents

Organizing and managing paperwork and documents can be a daunting task, especially for individuals with hoarding disorder. The accumulation of papers and documents can contribute to the clutter and disorganization within their living space. In this chapter, we will explore strategies and techniques to effectively handle paperwork and documents, allowing for a more organized and clutter-free environment.

## THE CHALLENGE OF PAPER CLUTTER

Paper clutter is a common issue in many households, but for individuals with hoarding disorder, it can be overwhelming. The fear of discarding important information or the sentimental attachment to documents can lead to a reluctance to let go. As a result, papers pile up, causing further clutter and making it difficult to find what is needed when it is needed.

# Sorting and Categorizing

The first step in tackling paper clutter is to sort and categorize the documents. Set aside some time in a quiet and dedicated space to go through each piece of paper. Create categories that make sense for your specific situation, such as bills, financial documents, medical records, and personal correspondence. As you sort through the papers, determine which ones are truly necessary to keep. Ask yourself if the document can be easily replaced or accessed digitally. For example, many financial institutions provide online statements, eliminating the need to keep hard copies. Consider shredding or recycling documents that are no longer needed.

# Establishing an Organizational System

After sorting and discarding unnecessary documents, it's important to establish an organizational system for the remaining ones. Start by investing in a filing cabinet or file box with clearly labeled folders. Assign each category of documents to a specific folder, making it easier to locate them when needed. Within each folder, consider using dividers or subfolders to further organize the documents. Label each section to provide clear distinction between different types of paperwork. For example, within the ''bills'' folder, you may have subsections for utilities, credit cards, and mortgage payments.

# Digitalizing Documents

In today's digital age, it is becoming increasingly easier to store and access important documents digitally. Consider scanning and saving important papers onto your computer or an external hard drive. This not only reduces physical clutter but also provides a backup in case the original document is lost or damaged. When digitizing documents, create folders and subfolders on your computer that mirror your physical filing system. Use clear and descriptive names for each document to make searching easier. If possible, consider using a cloud storage service to ensure that your files are securely backed up and accessible from anywhere.

# Regular Maintenance

Once you have established an organizational system for your paperwork and documents, it's crucial to maintain it consistently. Dedicate a regular time slot each week or month to review and file any new papers that have accumulated.

This preventive maintenance will prevent the clutter from building up again and make it easier to find what you need when you need it. Additionally, consider implementing a system for dealing with incoming mail and other documents. Designate a specific spot, such as a mail tray or designated inbox, to place all incoming papers. Set aside time regularly to go through these papers, sort them into appropriate categories, and file them accordingly.

# BENEFITS OF DECLUTTERING PAPERWORK

Decluttering and organizing paperwork can provide several benefits for individuals with hoarding disorder. It reduces visual clutter, creating a more peaceful and relaxing environment. It also improves productivity and decreases stress by making it easier to find important documents when needed. Furthermore, decluttering paperwork can help individuals gain a sense of control over their living space and reduce overall anxiety.

# SEEKING SUPPORT

Managing paper clutter can be a challenging task, and it is important to seek support if needed. Consider reaching out to a professional organizer or a trusted friend or family member who can provide guidance and encouragement throughout the process. Remember, you don't have to tackle paper clutter alone, and seeking support can make the journey to a clutter-free space more manageable.

# CONCLUSION

Handling paperwork and documents is an essential part of decluttering for individuals with hoarding disorder. By sorting and categorizing papers, establishing an organizational system, digitalizing documents, and maintaining regular maintenance, individuals can overcome paper clutter and create a more organized living environment. Seek support and approach the task with patience, and soon you will experience the benefits of a clutter-free and streamlined paperwork system.

# Chapter 17: Dealing with Cluttered Spaces

Dealing with cluttered spaces is a crucial step in overcoming hoarding disorder. When the accumulation of possessions reaches a point where they have taken over living spaces, it can create safety hazards, impede daily activities, and contribute to feelings of overwhelm and stress. It's important to address cluttered spaces in order to create a functional and organized living environment.

## UNDERSTANDING THE IMPACT OF CLUTTER

Clutter can have a profound impact on our physical and mental well-being. Living in a cluttered space can make it difficult to find the things we need, increase stress levels, and reduce productivity. It can also create feelings of shame and embarrassment, particularly when it comes to inviting others into our homes. Cluttered spaces can also pose safety risks, such as tripping hazards or difficulty accessing emergency exits. Excessive clutter can lead to poor air quality and an increased risk of pests or mold. Addressing cluttered spaces is not only important for improving psychological well-being but also for ensuring a safe and healthy living environment.

# DEVELOPING A PLAN OF ACTION

Dealing with cluttered spaces requires a systematic approach. Instead of attempting to tackle the entire space at once, break it down into smaller, more manageable tasks. This helps to prevent overwhelm and allows for a sense of accomplishment as each task is completed. Start by identifying the areas in your home that are most cluttered. This could be a specific room, a closet, or even just a small corner. Prioritize these areas based on their impact on daily functioning and emotional well-being. By starting with smaller, less overwhelming spaces, you can build momentum and confidence as you progress.

# SORTING AND CATEGORIZING BELONGINGS

Once you've identified the areas to tackle, it's important to develop a system for sorting and categorizing belongings. This helps to streamline the decluttering process and makes it easier to determine which items to keep, donate, or discard. Create designated piles or containers for different categories, such as "keep," "donate," and "discard." As you go through each item, ask yourself crucial questions: Do I use this item? Does it bring me joy or serve a purpose in my life? Am I holding onto it out of guilt or obligation? Be honest with yourself and challenge any irrational beliefs or attachments you may have to possessions. Remember, the goal is to create a clutter-free living space that is functional and supports your overall well-being. This may require making difficult decisions and letting go of items that no longer serve you. But by doing so, you create space for new experiences and a more balanced lifestyle.

## SEEKING SUPPORT

Dealing with cluttered spaces can feel overwhelming, and it's important to seek support throughout the process. Reach out to loved ones who can provide encouragement and assistance. Consider joining a support group or seeking the guidance of a professional organizer or therapist specializing in hoarding disorder. Support from others can provide accountability and help you stay motivated during the decluttering process. They can also provide a fresh perspective and offer guidance on organization strategies that may work best for your specific situation.

# MAINTAINING A CLUTTER-FREE ENVIRONMENT

Once you've successfully dealt with cluttered spaces, it's important to establish habits and systems to maintain a clutter-free environment. Implementing daily routines such as cleaning, tidying up, and organizing can help prevent clutter from accumulating again. Regular maintenance involves disciplining yourself to put things back where they belong, establishing a designated space for each item, and resisting the urge to acquire unnecessary possessions. It's important to recognize that maintaining a clutter-free environment is an ongoing process that requires commitment and effort. By consistently practicing clutter management strategies, you can cultivate a sense of peace and well-being in your home. A clutter-free space not only improves your physical environment but also has a positive impact on your mental and emotional state.

# Takeaways

- Dealing with cluttered spaces is crucial for overcoming hoarding disorder and creating a functional living environment. - Clutter can have a negative impact on physical and mental well-being. - Break down decluttering tasks into smaller, more manageable steps. - Develop a system for sorting and categorizing belongings. - Seek support from loved ones, support groups, or professionals. - Establish habits and routines to maintain a clutter-free environment. - Remember that maintaining a clutter-free environment is an ongoing process. In the next chapter, we will delve into creating functional living spaces and explore various organizing systems and strategies.

# Chapter 18: Creating Functional Living Spaces

Creating functional living spaces is an essential step in the process of decluttering and organizing. When dealing with hoarding disorder, it's common for living spaces to become overwhelmed with possessions, making it difficult to navigate and utilize the area effectively. This chapter will provide strategies and tips for transforming cluttered spaces into functional and organized environments.

# THE IMPORTANCE OF FUNCTIONAL LIVING SPACES

Living in a cluttered environment can have a significant impact on our daily lives. It can impede our ability to complete tasks efficiently and comfortably, create a sense of overwhelm and anxiety, and hinder social interactions. By creating functional living spaces, we can enhance our overall well-being and regain control over our surroundings.

## Assessing the Space

The first step in creating functional living spaces is to assess the current state of the area. Take a moment to evaluate the room or rooms that are most affected by clutter. Consider the layout, available storage options, and any specific challenges that need to be addressed.

## Designate Areas and Zones

Once you've assessed the space, it's time to designate specific areas and zones for different activities. This will help create a sense of order and structure within the room. For example, you can have a designated reading corner, workspace, and relaxation area. By assigning specific purposes to different parts of the room, you'll be able to navigate the area more easily and efficiently.

# Utilize Storage Solutions

Storage solutions are crucial in creating functional living spaces. They help maximize space and keep belongings organized and easily accessible. Consider incorporating storage containers, shelves, and bins that fit the overall aesthetic of the room. Utilize vertical space by installing shelves on walls or using hanging storage solutions. Remember to label containers to make it easier to find and maintain the organization.

# Streamline Belongings

Creating functional living spaces requires decluttering and streamlining belongings. Take the time to sort through your possessions and determine what is essential and what can be let go of. Letting go of items that no longer serve a purpose or bring joy can create more space and reduce clutter. Be mindful of your emotional attachments and make decisions based on what will contribute to a functional and organized space.

# Simplify Furniture Arrangement

Consider the furniture arrangement in the room. Simplify the layout by removing unnecessary furniture or reducing the number of pieces. Allow for ample space to move around and ensure that furniture serves its intended purpose. Rearrange furniture to create flow and prioritize functionality over cluttered arrangements.

# Establish Clear Pathways

Cluttered spaces often lack clear pathways, making it challenging to navigate the room. Ensure that there are clear and unobstructed pathways throughout the living space. This will enhance the ease of movement and prevent accidents or injuries. Remove any excessive furniture or belongings that obstruct the flow of the room.

# Create Visual Order

Visual order plays a vital role in creating functional living spaces. Organize belongings in a way that is visually appealing and contributes to a sense of calm and order. Use storage containers or shelving units to group items and create a cohesive look. Incorporate aesthetics that align with your personal style to make the space inviting and enjoyable.

## Maintain Organization

Creating functional living spaces is an ongoing process that requires regular maintenance. Establish daily or weekly routines to ensure that the organization is maintained. Take a few minutes each day to put items back in their designated places and declutter any accumulating mess. Regularly reassess the space and make adjustments as needed to accommodate changing needs.

## CONCLUSION

Creating functional living spaces is a transformative process that can significantly enhance our well-being and quality of life. By assessing the space, designating areas, utilizing storage solutions, streamlining belongings, simplifying furniture arrangements, establishing clear pathways, creating visual order, and maintaining organization, we can create a clutter-free and functional environment that supports our daily activities. Remember that the journey to functional living spaces requires patience, commitment, and ongoing maintenance, but the rewards are well worth the effort.

# Chapter 19: Cleaning and Sanitizing

Cleaning and sanitizing are essential steps in the decluttering process for individuals with hoarding disorder. Not only does a cluttered environment pose physical health risks, but it can also contribute to feelings of overwhelm and distress. By implementing effective cleaning and sanitizing practices, individuals can create a safer and more comfortable living space.

## THE IMPORTANCE OF CLEANING

Cleaning goes beyond simply tidying up and removing visible clutter. It involves deep cleaning and ensuring that the environment is free from dust, dirt, and potential allergens. Here are some key reasons why cleaning is important in the context of hoarding disorder:

# 1. Health and Safety:

A cluttered environment creates the perfect breeding ground for allergens, mold, and bacteria. Dust accumulation can trigger allergies and respiratory issues, while mold and bacteria can pose significant health risks. By regularly cleaning and removing debris, individuals can improve the overall air quality and reduce the risk of health complications.

# 2. Pest Control:

A cluttered and unclean environment attracts pests such as rodents, insects, and vermin. These pests can cause further damage to the property and pose health risks. Regular cleaning and proper disposal of food waste can help prevent pest infestations.

# 3. Organization and Functionality:

Cleaning allows individuals to create a more organized and functional living space. By removing excess clutter and cleaning the surfaces, individuals can find items more easily and navigate through their home with greater ease. Additionally, cleaning promotes a sense of pride and ownership over one's living environment.

# THE PROCESS OF CLEANING

Cleaning a cluttered space can feel overwhelming, but breaking it down into smaller tasks can make it more manageable. Here is a step-by-step process to follow when cleaning a hoarded environment:

# 1. Prepare:

Gather the necessary cleaning supplies, such as gloves, masks, cleaning solutions, and garbage bags. It's important to use environmentally friendly and non-toxic cleaning products whenever possible.

# 2. Start Small:

Begin clearing cluttered areas one at a time. Focus on smaller spaces or specific items, such as countertops, tables, or shelves. This helps in creating a sense of accomplishment and prevents becoming overwhelmed.

# 3. Sort and Categorize:

As you clean, sort items into categories such as keep, donate, sell, or discard. This process helps in making decisions about what to keep and what to let go of. Remember to be mindful of sentimental items and allow yourself time to emotionally process the decision-making process.

# 4. Clean and Disinfect:

Once the clutter is removed, thoroughly clean and disinfect the surfaces. Use appropriate cleaning solutions for each surface, and pay attention to areas that may have been hidden under clutter for a long time. This step is crucial for eliminating germs and bacteria.

# 5. Declutter as You Go:

As you clean, continue decluttering by assessing the items you encounter. Ask yourself if each item is necessary or if it holds sentimental value. If an item no longer serves a purpose or brings you joy, consider letting it go.

# 6. Maintenance:

After the initial cleaning and decluttering process, establish a regular cleaning routine to maintain a clean and organized living space. Set a schedule for cleaning and stick to it, so clutter does not accumulate again.

# CLEANING SAFETY TIPS

When tackling a cluttered environment, it's important to prioritize safety. Here are some key tips to keep in mind:

## 1. Wear Protective Gear:

Use gloves, masks, and other protective gear to avoid potential health hazards, especially when working with mold, sharp objects, or chemicals.

## 2. Use Proper Cleaning Techniques:

Learn the correct cleaning techniques for different surfaces and materials to avoid causing damage. For example, use appropriate cleaning products and methods for wooden furniture, electronics, or delicate fabrics.

## 3. Take Breaks:

Cleaning a cluttered space can be physically and emotionally demanding. Take frequent breaks to rest and recharge.

## 4. Seek Professional Help:

If the clutter or cleaning process feels too overwhelming or unsafe, consider reaching out to professional cleaning services or experts who specialize in hoarding disorder.

## 5. Gradual Progress:

Remember that cleaning and decluttering is a gradual process. Be patient with yourself and celebrate small achievements along the way. Cleaning and sanitizing a hoarded environment takes time and effort, but it is an important step towards creating a safe and comfortable living space. By prioritizing health, organization, and safety, individuals with hoarding disorder can improve their overall well-being and enjoy the benefits of a clean and clutter-free environment.

# Chapter 20: Reducing Acquiring Behaviors

Acquiring behaviors play a significant role in hoarding disorder, as individuals with this condition have a strong tendency to acquire and accumulate possessions. This chapter explores strategies and techniques to help reduce acquiring behaviors and promote a clutter-free lifestyle.

# UNDERSTANDING ACQUIRING BEHAVIORS

Acquiring behaviors in hoarding disorder often stem from various underlying factors, including an intense need to acquire items, difficulty resisting urges to acquire, fear of missing out, and a belief that acquiring possessions will bring a sense of security or happiness. It is important to recognize that acquiring behaviors can become a compulsive and habitual pattern, reinforcing the cycle of hoarding.

# CHALLENGING BELIEFS AND ADDRESSING TRIGGERS

One of the first steps in reducing acquiring behaviors is to challenge the beliefs and thoughts associated with them. This involves questioning the belief that acquiring possessions will fulfill emotional needs or provide a sense of security. It is essential to explore alternative ways of finding comfort, security, and happiness that do not involve excessive acquisition. Identifying triggers for acquiring behaviors is also crucial. These triggers can include advertisements, sales, online shopping platforms, emotional distress, boredom, or social influences. By understanding the triggers, individuals can develop strategies to prevent or manage these situations effectively.

# DEVELOPING ALTERNATIVE COPING MECHANISMS

Reducing acquiring behaviors requires finding alternative coping mechanisms to deal with emotional distress or triggers. Instead of turning to acquiring possessions, individuals can explore healthier ways to manage stress, anxiety, or other negative emotions. This may involve engaging in physical exercise, practicing relaxation techniques, journaling, seeking support from loved ones, or engaging in hobbies that bring joy and fulfillment.

# SETTING LIMITS AND ESTABLISHING RULES

Creating rules and setting limits around acquiring can provide structure and guidance for individuals with hoarding disorder. This can include establishing a "one-in-one-out" rule, where for every new item acquired, one existing item must be discarded or donated. Implementing a waiting period before making a purchase can also help reduce impulsive buying. It is essential to develop a specific budget for acquiring items and stick to it. Financial constraints can help curb excessive shopping habits and provide a sense of control over acquiring behaviors.

# UTILIZING SUPPORT SYSTEMS

Having a support system is critical in reducing acquiring behaviors. Loved ones, friends, or support groups can provide encouragement, accountability, and assistance in challenging and changing the mindset around acquiring possessions. By sharing concerns and progress, individuals can find encouragement and motivation to stay committed to their goals.

# PROFESSIONAL HELP

Seeking professional help is highly recommended for individuals struggling with acquiring behaviors in hoarding disorder. Therapists or mental health professionals specializing in hoarding disorder can provide guidance, support, and evidence-based interventions to address acquiring behaviors effectively. Cognitive-behavioral therapy (CBT) and dialectical behavior therapy (DBT) are two approaches commonly used to target acquiring behaviors and modify related thought patterns.

# MONITORING PROGRESS AND CELEBRATING SUCCESSES

Reducing acquiring behaviors is an ongoing process that requires persistence and self-reflection. It is important to monitor progress and celebrate even small successes along the way. Recognizing achievements, no matter how minor, can help boost motivation and reinforce positive change.

# ACHIEVING A CLUTTER-FREE LIFE

By reducing acquiring behaviors, individuals can work towards achieving a clutter-free life. This involves consciously practicing the strategies discussed in this chapter, seeking support, and embracing a mindset shift towards valuing experiences and connections over material possessions. Remember, it is a journey, and each step taken brings individuals closer to a more fulfilling and clutter-free life. Remember, reducing acquiring behaviors is a process that requires dedication, perseverance, and patience. With the right strategies and support, individuals can overcome hoarding disorder and create a healthier relationship with possessions.

# Chapter 21: Addressing Hoarding Behaviors at the Source

In order to effectively address hoarding behaviors, it is essential to understand and tackle the root causes. Hoarding disorder is a complex mental health condition that is influenced by various factors, including genetic, environmental, and psychological elements. By addressing these underlying causes, individuals can make significant progress in overcoming their hoarding behaviors and creating lasting change.

## GENETIC FACTORS

Research suggests that genetics plays a role in hoarding disorder. Individuals with first-degree relatives who hoard have an increased likelihood of developing the disorder themselves. Certain genes may make it difficult for individuals to regulate their emotions and make decisions about acquiring and discarding possessions. Understanding the genetic factors at play can provide valuable insight into an individual's hoarding behaviors and help tailor their treatment approach.

# ENVIRONMENTAL INFLUENCES

Childhood experiences and exposure to trauma can also contribute to hoarding behaviors. Individuals who grew up in cluttered or chaotic households may develop hoarding tendencies as a way to cope with the chaos and instability they experienced. Additionally, societal and cultural influences, such as material wealth and accumulation, can fuel hoarding behaviors. It is important to recognize and address these environmental influences in order to effectively tackle hoarding behaviors.

# PSYCHOLOGICAL FACTORS

Underlying mental health conditions can contribute to hoarding disorder. Conditions such as anxiety, depression, obsessive-compulsive disorder (OCD), and attention-deficit/hyperactivity disorder (ADHD) are often present alongside hoarding behaviors. Trauma and past experiences can also shape hoarding behaviors, as possessions may provide a sense of comfort, security, or control. Understanding and addressing these psychological factors is essential in developing effective treatment strategies.

## SEEKING PROFESSIONAL HELP

Addressing hoarding behaviors at the source often requires the guidance and support of mental health professionals. Therapists and psychologists can help individuals explore the underlying causes of their hoarding disorder and develop coping strategies to manage it. Therapy may involve discussing past experiences, thought patterns, and triggers for hoarding behaviors. By working with professionals, individuals can gain a deeper understanding of themselves and their behaviors, leading to lasting change.

# CULTIVATING SELF-REFLECTION

In addition to seeking professional help, cultivating self-reflection is a valuable practice for addressing hoarding behaviors at the source. Journaling, mindfulness practices, and self-care activities can provide insight into the origins of hoarding behaviors and help individuals explore their thoughts and emotions surrounding possessions. Approaching self-reflection with self-compassion and patience allows individuals to gain a better understanding of themselves, their motivations, and their relationship with their possessions. Addressing hoarding behaviors at the source is an ongoing and dynamic process that requires self-exploration, professional guidance, and a commitment to personal growth. By understanding the genetic, environmental, and psychological factors that contribute to hoarding disorder, individuals can develop personalized strategies to overcome their hoarding behaviors and create a clutter-free life.

# Chapter 22: Overcoming Emotional Attachments

## UNDERSTANDING EMOTIONAL ATTACHMENTS

Hoarding disorder is often driven by emotional attachments to possessions. These attachments can be deep-rooted and difficult to overcome, but it is possible to develop healthier relationships with belongings and let go of unnecessary items. Understanding the nature of emotional attachments is the first step in this process. Emotional attachments to possessions often stem from the sentimental value we assign to them. These items hold memories, represent certain periods in our lives, or serve as a connection to loved ones. They can evoke strong emotions and a sense of comfort and security. Additionally, emotional attachments can be fueled by fear and anxiety. Individuals with hoarding disorder may worry that letting go of an item will cause them to lose a part of themselves, lose the memories associated with the item, or regret the decision in the future. These fears can create a sense of urgency to hold onto possessions, leading to clutter and disorganization.

# SHIFTING PERSPECTIVES

To overcome emotional attachments, it is important to shift our perspectives on possessions. We must reframe our thoughts and beliefs about the value and significance of these items. Here are some strategies to help with this process: 1. Reflect on the significance: Take a step back and reflect on why a particular item holds emotional importance for you. Is it truly the item itself or the memories and emotions associated with it? Recognize that memories can be cherished and preserved without the physical presence of the item. 2. Prioritize what truly matters: Identify the possessions that truly hold value and meaning in your life. Consider the impact they have on your overall well-being and the functionality of your space. Let go of items that do not contribute to your happiness or serve a practical purpose. 3. Create a memory box: If there are items that you find difficult to part with completely, consider creating a memory box. In this box, you can store a select few sentimental items that hold significant emotional value. The key is to limit the number of items in the box and be selective about what you choose to keep. 4. Digitalize memories: In today's digital age, it is easier than ever to preserve memories without the physical clutter. Take photographs or scan important documents and store them in a digital format. This way, you can still access and cherish these memories without the need for physical possessions. 5. Seek support: Overcoming emotional attachments can be challenging, and it may be helpful to seek support from a therapist, support group, or loved ones. Talking about your feelings and concerns with others who understand can provide valuable perspective and encouragement. 6. Practice gradual release: If the thought of letting go of certain items is overwhelming, try practicing gradual release. Start small by letting go of a few less sentimental possessions and gradually work your way towards items that hold deeper emotional attachments. This step-by-step approach can make the process more manageable and less daunting. 7. Letting go ceremony: Consider holding a letting go ceremony to symbolically release the emotional attachments to possessions. This could involve writing a letter to the item, expressing gratitude for the memories it represents, and then letting it go through donation or discarding. Creating a ritual around letting go can provide closure and a sense of empowerment.

# PATIENCE AND COMPASSION

Overcoming emotional attachments is a journey that requires patience, self-compassion, and understanding. It is important to be gentle with yourself throughout this process and recognize that change takes time. Remember that possessions do not define your identity or worth. Letting go of emotional attachments can create space for new experiences, relationships, and personal growth. Embrace the opportunities that come with a clutter-free and organized living environment and celebrate the progress you make along the way.

# Chapter 23: Building Healthy Coping Mechanisms

In the journey towards overcoming hoarding disorder, building healthy coping mechanisms is a crucial step. Coping mechanisms are strategies and techniques that individuals utilize to manage stress, regulate emotions, and navigate difficult situations. For individuals with hoarding disorder, developing effective coping mechanisms is essential in reducing the reliance on hoarding behaviors and creating healthier ways of dealing with emotions and life challenges.

# THE ROLE OF COPING MECHANISMS IN HOARDING DISORDER

Hoarding disorder often develops as a way to cope with various emotional and psychological distress. As individuals accumulate possessions, they believe that these items provide comfort, security, and a sense of control. However, hoarding behaviors ultimately lead to more distress, as the clutter and disorganization cause negative impacts on daily functioning and overall well-being. Building healthy coping mechanisms is essential for breaking this cycle and addressing the underlying emotional needs that drive hoarding behaviors. By developing alternative strategies for managing emotions and stress, individuals can gradually reduce their reliance on hoarding and create a more balanced and fulfilling life.

# IDENTIFYING UNHEALTHY COPING MECHANISMS

Before building healthy coping mechanisms, it is important to identify and understand the unhealthy ones that contribute to hoarding disorder. Some common unhealthy coping mechanisms may include:

## 1. Avoidance:

Individuals may avoid addressing challenging emotions or situations by distracting themselves with excessive acquiring or immersing themselves in cluttered environments.

## 2. Emotional Avoidance:

Instead of facing and processing difficult emotions, individuals may suppress or numb their feelings through hoarding behaviors. The accumulation of possessions can serve as a buffer against emotional pain.

## 3. Perfectionism:

Feelings of anxiety and fear of making mistakes can drive individuals to hoard, as they believe that keeping everything can prevent potential future problems and errors.

# 4. Emotional Attachments:

Hoarding behaviors may be fueled by strong emotional attachments to possessions, leading individuals to avoid parting with items due to sentimentality and fear of losing memories or connections.

# 5. Escapism:

Turning to the cluttered environment as a means of escape from the outside world and its stressors can perpetuate hoarding behaviors.

## DEVELOPING HEALTHY COPING MECHANISMS

Building healthy coping mechanisms requires self-reflection, self-awareness, and a willingness to explore and adopt new strategies. Here are some effective coping mechanisms that can help individuals overcome hoarding disorder:

# 1. Emotional Awareness:

Developing awareness of emotions is crucial in managing them effectively. Recognizing and acknowledging emotions as they arise can help individuals address them in healthier ways.

# 2. Mindfulness:

Practicing mindfulness techniques, such as deep breathing exercises, meditation, and grounding techniques, can help individuals stay present and reduce anxiety and stress. Mindfulness helps cultivate a non-judgmental awareness of thoughts, emotions, and physical sensations.

# 3. Stress Management:

Finding healthy outlets to manage stress is essential in reducing the reliance on hoarding behaviors. Engaging in activities such as exercise, hobbies, spending time in nature, or practicing relaxation techniques can help individuals regulate their stress levels effectively.

# 4. Assertive Communication:

Developing assertive communication skills can help individuals express their needs, set boundaries, and ask for support when needed. Effective communication can reduce the feelings of overwhelm and help individuals navigate relationships more effectively.

## 5. Self-Compassion:

Practicing self-compassion involves treating oneself with kindness, understanding, and acceptance. It is important to acknowledge that overcoming hoarding disorder is a journey and that setbacks or challenges are a normal part of the process.

## 6. Healthy Habits:

Establishing a routine that includes healthy habits, such as regular exercise, balanced nutrition, sufficient sleep, and self-care activities, can support overall well-being and contribute to emotional stability.

## SEEKING PROFESSIONAL SUPPORT

Building healthy coping mechanisms may require professional guidance and support. Mental health professionals, such as therapists and psychologists, can provide valuable insights, tools, and techniques to help individuals develop and implement effective coping strategies. Therapy sessions can provide a safe space to explore underlying emotions, experiences, and thought patterns that contribute to hoarding behaviors.

# SUMMARY

Building healthy coping mechanisms is a crucial step in overcoming hoarding disorder. Individuals who struggle with hoarding behaviors often turn to unhealthy coping mechanisms that perpetuate the cycle of hoarding and emotional distress. By identifying these unhealthy coping mechanisms and instilling healthier strategies, such as emotional awareness, mindfulness, stress management, assertive communication, self-compassion, and healthy habits, individuals can create positive changes in their lives. Seeking professional support can be instrumental in this process, providing guidance and personalized strategies for building healthy coping mechanisms.

# Chapter 24: Developing a Support Network

Developing a strong support network is essential for individuals with hoarding disorder on their path to recovery. Hoarding disorder can often leave individuals feeling isolated and overwhelmed, making it crucial to have a network of people who understand and offer support.

## THE IMPORTANCE OF A SUPPORT NETWORK

Having a support network can provide various benefits for individuals with hoarding disorder. Here are some key reasons why developing a support network is important: 1. Emotional Support: Dealing with hoarding disorder can be emotionally challenging, and having a network of understanding and empathetic individuals can provide much-needed emotional support. These individuals can listen and offer encouragement, helping to alleviate feelings of isolation and shame. 2. Practical Help: Hoarding disorder often involves intensive decluttering and organizing efforts. Having people who are willing to lend a hand and offer practical help can make the decluttering process more manageable and less overwhelming. 3. Accountability: A support network can help hold individuals accountable for their actions and goals. They can provide gentle reminders, offer motivation, and help individuals stay on track with their decluttering and organizing efforts. 4. Perspective: Supportive individuals can offer fresh perspectives and provide insights that individuals with hoarding disorder may not have considered. They can provide guidance and suggestions for effective decluttering strategies and organizing systems. 5. Encouragement: Overcoming hoarding disorder requires perseverance and commitment. Having a support network that offers continuous encouragement and celebrates small victories can help individuals stay motivated and focused on their recovery journey.

# BUILDING A SUPPORT NETWORK

Building a support network may involve reaching out to various individuals and resources. Here are some strategies to help develop a strong support system: 1. Family and Friends: Begin by confiding in family members and close friends who can provide emotional support and understanding. Share your experiences, challenges, and goals with them, and let them know how they can support you on your journey. 2. Mental Health Professionals: Seek the assistance of mental health professionals who specialize in hoarding disorder. They can provide guidance, therapy, and valuable coping strategies tailored to your specific needs. Therapists, psychologists, and counselors can play a vital role in your recovery process. 3. Support Groups: Consider joining support groups specifically for hoarding disorder. These groups provide a safe and non-judgmental environment where you can share your experiences, learn from others, and gain valuable insights and strategies for coping with hoarding disorder. 4. Professional Organizers: Engage the services of professional organizers experienced in dealing with hoarding disorder. They can provide practical assistance, support, and guidance in the decluttering and organizing process. 5. Online Communities: Join online communities or forums dedicated to hoarding disorder. These platforms can provide a sense of community and connection with others who are going through similar experiences. Engage in discussions, seek advice, and share your progress and challenges.

# MAINTAINING A SUPPORT NETWORK

Building a support network is an ongoing process that requires effort and maintenance. Here are some tips for maintaining a strong support system: 1. Regular Communication: Stay in touch with your support network regularly. Whether it's through frequent phone calls, meetings, or online interactions, maintaining open lines of communication is crucial for receiving ongoing support and encouragement. 2. Be Honest and Vulnerable: Be open and honest about your feelings and struggles with your support network. Sharing your challenges and fears will allow them to understand your needs better and provide appropriate support. 3. Attend Support Group Meetings: Regularly participate in support group meetings or therapy sessions. These sessions offer an opportunity to share experiences, gain insights, and receive encouragement from others facing similar challenges. 4. Express Gratitude: Take the time to express gratitude to your support network. Acknowledge and appreciate the individuals who have been there for you, offering support and encouragement throughout your journey. 5. Seek Professional Help When Needed: If you find yourself struggling or facing setbacks, don't hesitate to seek professional help. Mental health professionals can provide guidance, reassess treatment plans, and offer additional support as necessary. Remember, building a support network takes time, patience, and effort. Be open to receiving help and support, and remember that you don't have to navigate the challenges of hoarding disorder alone. With a strong support network by your side, you can find the encouragement and guidance needed to overcome hoarding disorder and embrace a clutter-free life. Next Chapter: Chapter 25: Seeking Professional Help

# Chapter 25: Seeking Professional Help

Seeking professional help is a crucial step in overcoming hoarding disorder. It is a complex mental health condition that requires specialized support and guidance from trained professionals. They can provide the expertise, tools, and techniques necessary to address the underlying causes of hoarding behavior and support individuals on their journey towards a clutter-free life.

# WHY SEEK PROFESSIONAL HELP?

1. Expertise: Mental health professionals, such as therapists and psychologists, have the expertise and knowledge to assess and diagnose hoarding disorder. They are trained to understand the complexities of this condition and can provide individualized treatment plans. 2. Understanding and Compassion: Hoarding disorder often remains hidden or undisclosed due to shame, embarrassment, and fear of judgment. Mental health professionals are trained to approach hoarding disorder with empathy, understanding, and non-judgmental attitudes. They create a safe and supportive environment for individuals to open up and share their experiences. 3. Assessment and Diagnosis: Seeking professional help allows for a comprehensive assessment and accurate diagnosis of hoarding disorder. This ensures that the right treatment approach is implemented based on the unique needs of the individual. 4. Tailored Treatment: Each person's journey towards recovery is different, and a qualified professional can provide tailored treatment plans that address the specific challenges and needs of individuals with hoarding

disorder. They can offer a combination of therapy, counseling, and support to help individuals break free from hoarding behaviors. 5. Behavioural Strategies: Mental health professionals can help individuals develop effective coping mechanisms and behavioral strategies to regulate emotions, manage stress, and reduce impulsive acquiring tendencies. These strategies are essential in navigating the difficulties of decluttering and maintaining a clutter-free lifestyle. 6. Holistic Approach: Professional help often involves a holistic approach to treatment, addressing both the mental health aspects of hoarding disorder and the physical clutter in the environment. Professionals can guide individuals in creating practical routines, organizing systems, and maintaining a clutter-free living space. 7. Progress Monitoring: Mental health professionals play a vital role in monitoring progress and providing ongoing support. They help individuals set achievable goals, track their progress, and offer guidance during challenging times. The journey to recovery can be challenging, but with the support of a professional, individuals can stay motivated and maintain their progress.

# HOW TO FIND PROFESSIONAL HELP?

1. Referrals: Start by reaching out to your primary care doctor or therapist for referrals to professionals who specialize in hoarding disorder. They may be able to recommend reputable mental health professionals experienced in treating hoarding disorder. 2. Online Directories: Utilize online directories or websites dedicated to mental health professionals. These platforms allow you to search for professionals in your area who specialize in hoarding disorder or related conditions. 3. Support Groups: Attend support groups specifically focused on hoarding disorder. These groups often have connections to professionals or can provide recommendations based on their own experiences. 4. Local Mental Health Organizations: Reach out to local mental health organizations or advocacy groups that specialize in hoarding disorder. They may have resources and recommendations for professionals who have expertise in this area. 5. Professional Organizers: Professional organizers who specialize in hoarding disorder can provide guidance and support in decluttering and organizing environments. They often have

connections to mental health professionals who can provide the necessary therapy and counseling. Remember, finding the right professional for your needs may require some research and trial-and-error. Be open to exploring different options and don't be afraid to ask questions or voice any concerns during the initial consultation. Building a strong therapeutic relationship with your mental health professional is vital for your progress and recovery.

# THE BENEFITS OF PROFESSIONAL HELP

Seeking professional help for hoarding disorder offers numerous benefits: 1. Validation and Understanding: Professionals offer validation and understanding, creating a safe space for individuals to share their struggles and experiences without judgment or shame. 2. Targeted Treatment: Professionals can devise personalized treatment plans that address the specific challenges and underlying causes of hoarding disorder, increasing the likelihood of successful recovery. 3. Support and Guidance: Professionals provide ongoing support and guidance throughout the decluttering process, helping individuals navigate the emotions and challenges that arise. 4. Coping Strategies: Therapists and psychologists can teach individuals effective coping strategies to manage emotions, reduce acquiring behaviors, and maintain a clutter-free lifestyle. 5. Motivation and Accountability: Professionals act as a source of motivation and accountability, helping individuals stay on track and celebrate their progress. 6. Relapse Prevention: Professionals can provide strategies and tools for maintaining progress and preventing relapse, ensuring long-term success in overcoming hoarding disorder. Remember, seeking professional help is a sign of strength, not weakness. It is an essential step towards reclaiming control over your life and creating a clutter-free environment that promotes well-being and happiness.

# Chapter 26: Maintaining Progress and Relapse Prevention

Congratulations on your progress towards decluttering your mind and environment! In this chapter, we will discuss the importance of maintaining the progress you have made and strategies to prevent relapse. Remember, this journey towards a clutter-free life is an ongoing process, and it requires consistent effort and commitment.

# THE IMPORTANCE OF MAINTENANCE

Maintaining the progress you have made is crucial to prevent reverting back to old hoarding behaviors. It ensures that all your hard work and effort do not go to waste. By establishing a maintenance routine, you can create a lasting change in your life. Regular maintenance helps you stay organized, keeps the clutter at bay, and ensures that your mind and environment remain in order. It also prevents the accumulation of new possessions and helps you make conscious decisions about what items to bring into your home.

# Developing a Maintenance Plan

To establish an effective maintenance plan, consider the following steps: 1. **Assess the Environment:** Take a step back and evaluate your surroundings. Identify any areas that require attention and prioritize your tasks. 2. **Break Tasks into Manageable Chunks:** Rather than overwhelming yourself with a large decluttering session, break down your tasks into smaller, more manageable chunks. Focus on one area at a time to avoid feeling overwhelmed. 3. **Set Realistic Goals:** Set achievable goals for yourself. Remember, maintaining progress is an ongoing process, and it's essential to set realistic expectations for yourself. 4. **Create a Schedule:** Develop a schedule that works best for you. Dedicate specific time slots or days of the week to tackle maintenance tasks. Consistency is key! 5. **Utilize Reminders and Checklists:** Use reminders and checklists to keep you on track. These can be helpful reminders to complete specific tasks or prompts to review your maintenance plan regularly.

## Strategies to Maintain Motivation

Maintaining motivation is crucial for long-term progress. Here are some strategies to help you stay motivated: 1. **Visualize the Ideal Living Space:** Imagine and visualize your clutter-free, organized living space. Keep this image in mind as a reminder of why you started this journey. 2. **Celebrate Small Wins:** Celebrate every small accomplishment along the way. Recognize and acknowledge your progress, no matter how minor it may seem. Rewards can reinforce positive behavior and keep you motivated. 3. **Seek Support:** Surround yourself with a supportive network of friends, family, or support groups. Share your progress and challenges with them. They can provide encouragement, accountability, and understanding. 4. **Reflect on Progress:** Take time to reflect on how far you've come. Reviewing your progress can be a powerful reminder of the positive changes you have made. 5. **Be Kind to Yourself:** Remember, setbacks are a normal part of the journey. If you experience a relapse, be gentle with yourself, and use it as an opportunity to learn and grow. Practice self-compassion and understand that change takes time.

## Preventing Relapse

While relapse can be discouraging, it is essential to approach it with a growth mindset. Here are some tips to help prevent relapse: 1. **Identify Triggers:** Take note of situations, emotions, or thoughts that may trigger hoarding tendencies. Awareness of these triggers can help you develop proactive strategies to manage them. 2. **Practice Self-Care:** Engage in self-care activities that promote emotional well-being and stress reduction. This may include practicing mindfulness, engaging in hobbies, exercising, or spending time in nature. 3. **Stay Connected to**

**Your Support Network:** Maintain regular communication with your support network. Reach out to them during challenging times or when you feel the urge to hoard. Remember, you don't have to face this journey alone. 4. **Regularly Review Your Maintenance Plan:** Set aside time periodically to review and adjust your maintenance plan. This will help you stay organized and ensure that you are on track with your decluttering goals. 5. **Seek Professional Help When Needed:** If you find yourself struggling to maintain progress or experiencing significant distress, don't hesitate to reach out to a mental health professional. They can provide guidance, support, and additional strategies to prevent relapse. Remember, maintaining progress and preventing relapse is an ongoing process. Embrace it as an opportunity for personal growth and a chance to create lasting change in your life. By staying committed, seeking support, and being patient with yourself, you can continue on the path towards a clutter-free and fulfilling life.

# Chapter 27: Hoarding in Relationships and Families

Relationships and family dynamics can be profoundly affected when one person in the family has hoarding disorder. The excessive clutter and disorganization can create tension, strain, and conflict within relationships. Understanding the impact of hoarding disorder on relationships and families is essential for fostering compassion, support, and effective communication.

# THE IMPACT ON RELATIONSHIPS

Hoarding disorder can strain relationships with partners, family members, and close friends. The excessive clutter and disorganization can make it challenging for individuals with hoarding disorder to maintain functional living spaces. This can lead to frustration and anger from loved ones who may feel overwhelmed or excluded from the living environment. The strain caused by hoarding disorder may result in tension, arguments, and a breakdown in communication. Loved ones may feel helpless or unable to understand why someone they care about cannot simply clean up or let go of possessions. This disconnect can create a sense of isolation and further strain the relationship. In some cases, hoarding disorder can lead to a loss of trust. Loved ones may feel deceived or betrayed if they discover the extent of the hoarder's clutter and were unaware of the severity. This loss of trust can make it difficult for both parties to navigate and address the underlying issues.

# SUPPORT AND COMMUNICATION

When hoarding disorder is present within a relationship or family, it is crucial to approach the situation with empathy, understanding, and open communication. Supporting a loved one with hoarding disorder requires patience, compassion, and a commitment to effective communication. Here are some strategies to navigate hoarding within relationships and families: 1. Education and Awareness: Take the time to educate yourself and your loved ones about hoarding disorder. Understanding the complexities of the condition can help reduce stigma, increase empathy, and foster understanding. 2. Open and Non-judgmental Communication: Create a safe space for open and honest communication. Encourage your loved one with hoarding disorder to express their thoughts and feelings without fear of judgment or criticism. Active listening and validation can help build trust and promote healthier communication. 3. Focus on the Person, Not the Hoard: It is essential to separate the individual from their possessions. Remember that hoarding disorder is a mental health condition and not a personal choice. Show empathy and compassion for the person beneath the clutter, and avoid blaming or shaming them. 4. Boundary Setting: Establish boundaries and expectations regarding the hoarding behavior. Clearly communicate your concerns and the impact of the clutter on your relationship or family dynamics. Work together to find common ground and compromises that respect both parties' needs and boundaries. 5. Seek Professional Help: Encourage your loved one with hoarding disorder to seek professional help. A therapist or counselor with experience in hoarding disorder can provide guidance, support, and strategies for managing the condition. Additionally, therapy can help address underlying emotional issues that contribute to hoarding behaviors. 6. Support Groups: Connect with support groups or organizations that specialize in hoarding disorder. These groups can offer a sense of community, understanding, and shared experiences. Attend group meetings together or individually to gain insights and support.

# INTERVENTIONS AND FAMILY MEETINGS

In some cases, a formal intervention or family meeting may be necessary to address the hoarding behavior and its impact on relationships and family dynamics. During an intervention or family meeting, loved ones come together in a supportive and non-judgmental way to express their concerns and offer help. When planning an intervention or family meeting, consider the following: 1. Educate Yourself: Learn about effective intervention strategies, emotional support, and resources available for individuals with hoarding disorder. 2. Choose the Right Time and Place: Select a time and place where everyone can feel comfortable and safe. Ensure privacy and minimize distractions. 3. Express Concerns and Impact: Use "I" statements to express your concerns about the hoarding behavior and its impact on the relationship or family. Share specific examples of how the hoarding has affected you emotionally, physically, or socially. 4. Offer Help and Support: Communicate your willingness to support your loved one in their journey towards recovery. Provide information on available resources and offer assistance in seeking professional help or organizing support. 5. Establish Boundaries and Consequences: Clearly communicate your boundaries and the consequences that may arise if the hoarding behavior continues to negatively impact the relationship or family. Boundaries may include limitations on cluttered areas or expectations for maintaining a safe and functional living environment. Remember that interventions and family meetings should be approached with empathy, respect, and a focus on collaboration rather than blame. The goal is to support your loved one in their journey towards recovery and create a supportive environment for change. In conclusion, hoarding disorder can have a significant impact on relationships and family dynamics. Understanding the challenges and complexities of hoarding within relationships and families is essential for fostering compassion, support, and effective communication. By educating yourself, promoting open communication, setting boundaries, seeking professional help, and considering interventions or family meetings, you can provide the necessary support to your loved one while maintaining healthy relationships.

# Chapter 28: Helping a Loved One with Hoarding Disorder

Hoarding disorder not only affects the individuals who experience it firsthand but also has a significant impact on their loved ones. If you have a family member or friend who struggles with hoarding disorder, you may feel overwhelmed, frustrated, and unsure of how to help. It's essential to approach the situation with empathy, understanding, and knowledge to provide the support they need. In this chapter, we will explore strategies for helping a loved one with hoarding disorder.

## 1. EDUCATE YOURSELF

The first step in helping a loved one with hoarding disorder is to educate yourself about the condition. Learn about the signs, symptoms, and underlying causes of hoarding disorder. Understand that hoarding is a complex mental health issue and not a personal choice or a reflection of laziness or selfishness. By increasing your understanding, you can approach the situation with compassion and empathy.

# 2. COMMUNICATE WITH EMPATHY

When talking to your loved one about their hoarding, it's crucial to approach the conversation with empathy and understanding. Avoid judgmental language or blaming them for their behaviors. Instead, express your concern and offer emotional support. Let them know that you want to understand their struggles and help them find a solution. Active listening is vital during these conversations, allowing your loved one to express their emotions and concerns without interruption.

# 3. OFFER PRACTICAL SUPPORT

Helping a loved one with hoarding disorder involves providing practical support. Offer your assistance in decluttering and organizing their living space but remember to respect their boundaries and decisions. Focus on small, manageable tasks and break the process down into steps, so it feels less overwhelming. Encourage your loved one to be actively involved in the decluttering process and make decisions about what to keep or let go.

# 4. ENCOURAGE PROFESSIONAL HELP

Hoarding disorder is a complex issue that often requires professional intervention. Encourage your loved one to seek help from mental health professionals who specialize in hoarding disorder. Therapy can provide a safe space for your loved one to explore the underlying causes of their hoarding behaviors, develop coping strategies, and work towards a clutter-free life. Offer to assist them in finding a therapist or attending appointments.

# 5. SET BOUNDARIES

While providing support to your loved one, it's crucial to set healthy boundaries. Recognize that you cannot control their choices or force them to change. Avoid enabling their hoarding behaviors by not contributing to the clutter or acquiring more items on their behalf. Instead, focus on creating a supportive and non-judgmental environment where they feel safe to discuss their struggles and progress.

# 6. PRACTICE PATIENCE

Overcoming hoarding disorder is a long and challenging process. It's essential to practice patience and understanding throughout the journey. Recognize that change takes time and setbacks may occur. Celebrate small victories and acknowledge the progress your loved one makes. Be there for them during the ups and downs, providing continuous support and encouragement.

# 7. CARE FOR YOURSELF

Supporting a loved one with hoarding disorder can be emotionally and physically draining. It's crucial to prioritize self-care and seek support for yourself. Find a support group or therapist who specializes in hoarding disorder to help you process your feelings and cope with the challenges you may face. Take breaks when needed, and remember that you cannot provide effective support if you neglect your well-being.

# CONCLUSION

Helping a loved one with hoarding disorder requires patience, understanding, and empathy. By educating yourself, communicating with empathy, offering practical support, encouraging professional help, setting boundaries, practicing patience, and caring for yourself, you can be a valuable source of support for your loved one. Remember that change takes time, and your consistent presence and encouragement can make a significant difference in their journey towards a clutter-free life.

# Chapter 29: Finding Self-Compassion and Acceptance

Hoarding disorder is often accompanied by feelings of shame, guilt, and self-blame. Individuals with hoarding disorder may struggle with accepting themselves and their struggle with excessive possessions. However, finding self-compassion and acceptance is crucial for healing and moving towards a clutter-free life.

# THE IMPORTANCE OF SELF-COMPASSION

Self-compassion involves treating yourself with kindness, understanding, and acceptance, especially in the face of difficulties or mistakes. It is about recognizing your inherent worth and embracing your imperfections. When it comes to hoarding disorder, self-compassion can help you navigate the challenging journey of decluttering and organizing.

Here are some reasons why self-compassion is important:

# 1. Reducing Self-Judgment:

Self-compassion allows you to let go of self-judgment and criticism. Instead of berating yourself for your hoarding behaviors, you can acknowledge them with understanding and forgiveness. This mindset shift can create a space for growth and change.

# 2. Supporting Emotional Healing:

Hoarding disorder is often accompanied by emotional distress. Self-compassion can provide a nurturing environment for emotional healing. By offering yourself kindness and understanding, you can acknowledge and process the difficult emotions associated with hoarding disorder.

# 3. Encouraging Motivation:

Self-compassion can fuel motivation for change. When you approach yourself with kindness and acceptance, you are more likely to feel motivated to declutter and let go of excessive possessions. Self-compassion helps you recognize your intrinsic worth and the potential for a clutter-free and fulfilling life.

# 4. Building Resilience:

Hoarding disorder can be a challenging and complex condition to overcome. Self-compassion can help build resilience and provide the necessary strength to navigate setbacks and challenges along the way. It allows you to be gentle with yourself and bounce back from difficult moments.

## CULTIVATING SELF-COMPASSION

Cultivating self-compassion is an ongoing practice that requires patience and intention. Here are some strategies to help you cultivate self-compassion in your journey towards a clutter-free life:

# 1. Mindful Awareness:

Practice mindful awareness of your thoughts and emotions, especially those related to hoarding disorder.

Notice when self-judgment arises and intentionally shift towards self-compassionate thoughts. Treat yourself as you would a close friend or loved one.

# 2. Self-Kindness:

Practice acts of self-kindness regularly. Engage in activities that bring you joy and comfort. Treat yourself to moments of relaxation or self-care. Remember that self-compassion is not selfish; it is necessary for your well-being and recovery.

# 3. Affirmations and Mantras:

Develop affirmations and mantras that promote self-compassion. Repeat these affirmations to yourself whenever you find negative self-talk arising. Some examples may include: - "I am deserving of love and forgiveness." - "I am doing my best, and that is enough." - "I embrace my imperfections and learn from them."

# 4. Seeking Support:

Surround yourself with a supportive network of friends, family, or a support group. Share your challenges and progress with people who understand and provide non-judgmental support. Their encouragement and empathy can reinforce your journey towards self-compassion.

# THE POWER OF ACCEPTANCE

In addition to self-compassion, acceptance plays a crucial role in the process of overcoming hoarding disorder. Acceptance involves acknowledging your current reality and embracing it without judgment or resistance. It is about understanding that hoarding disorder does not define your worth as a person.

## The Benefits of Acceptance:

Acceptance can provide the following benefits:

### 1. Letting Go of Control:

Hoarding disorder often emerges as a way to gain a sense of control in life. However, acceptance allows you to let go of the need to control every aspect of your environment. It liberates you from the constant struggle against clutter and opens the door to a more balanced and peaceful life.

### 2. Embracing Imperfection:

Acceptance involves embracing imperfections, both in yourself and in your environment. It acknowledges that perfection is unattainable and that it is okay to have flaws and make mistakes. By accepting imperfection, you free yourself from the burden of unrealistic expectations.

### 3. Shifting Focus:

Acceptance enables you to shift your focus from the past or future to the present moment. It allows you to accept the reality of the clutter and engage in productive actions to declutter and organize. By accepting the current state, you can better direct your energy towards creating a clutter-free and fulfilling life.

### 4. Inner Peace and Well-Being:

Acceptance brings inner peace and well-being. It frees you from the constant struggle against your hoarding behaviors and allows space for self-growth and healing. Acceptance invites self-compassion and understanding, fostering a more positive and harmonious relationship with yourself.

# CONCLUSION

Finding self-compassion and acceptance are vital steps in the journey towards overcoming hoarding disorder. They provide the foundation for healing, growth, and a clutter-free life. Through self-compassion, you can develop a kind and nurturing relationship with yourself, while acceptance allows for the acknowledgment of the current reality and the possibility for positive transformation. Embrace self-compassion and acceptance as essential tools on your path to reclaiming control and finding joy in a clutter-free life.

# Chapter 30: Embracing a Clutter-Free Life

Living a clutter-free life is not just about having a neat and organized physical environment. It is a mindset shift and a commitment to a new way of living. In this final chapter, we will explore the benefits of embracing a clutter-free life, as well as practical strategies to help you maintain order and create a sense of peace and harmony in your surroundings.

## THE BENEFITS OF A CLUTTER-FREE LIFE

Embracing a clutter-free life has numerous benefits that extend beyond the physical environment. Let's take a closer look at some of these benefits: 1. Improved mental and emotional well-being: A clutter-free environment can have a positive impact on your mental and emotional health. It can reduce feelings of overwhelm, anxiety, and stress, allowing you to experience a greater sense of calm and clarity. 2. Increased productivity: When your physical space is organized and free from clutter, you can focus better and accomplish tasks more efficiently.

You'll spend less time searching for items and have more time and energy to devote to activities that are meaningful to you. 3. Enhanced creativity and inspiration: Clutter can be visually distracting and drain your mental energy. By clearing away the excess, you create space for inspiration and creativity to thrive. A clutter-free environment allows you to think more clearly and generate new ideas. 4. Better physical health: Cluttered spaces can be breeding grounds for dust, allergens, and pests, which can negatively impact your health. By maintaining a clutter-free home, you reduce the risk of allergies, respiratory issues, and other health concerns. 5. Strengthened relationships: A clutter-free living space can improve the quality of your relationships with family and friends. It creates an inviting and welcoming environment, making it easier for loved ones to visit and spend quality time with you.

# STRATEGIES FOR MAINTAINING A CLUTTER-FREE LIFE

Now that you understand the benefits of a clutter-free life, let's explore some strategies to help you maintain order and prevent clutter from accumulating: 1. Set realistic expectations:

Recognize that decluttering is an ongoing process, and it's natural for some clutter to accumulate over time. Set realistic expectations for yourself and kindly remind yourself that small slips or setbacks are a normal part of the journey. 2. Regular decluttering sessions: Schedule regular decluttering sessions to prevent clutter from building up. Set aside a specific time each week or month to assess your belongings and let go of anything that no longer serves you. 3. One in, one out policy: Implement a "one in, one out" policy for new items. For every new item you bring into your space, make a commitment to let go of something else. This helps maintain a balance and prevents clutter from piling up. 4. Practice mindful shopping: Before making a purchase, ask yourself if the item is truly necessary and if it aligns with your values and goals. Avoid impulse buying and instead focus on buying items that bring value and joy to your life. 5. Create designated storage spaces: Assign specific storage spaces for different categories of items. Clearly label containers and shelves to make it easier to locate items and maintain an organized environment. 6. Regular cleaning and maintenance: Dedicate time to regular cleaning and maintenance tasks, such as dusting, vacuuming, and wiping down surfaces. These routine tasks help keep your space clean and prevent clutter from accumulating. 7. Practice gratitude and contentment: Cultivate a mindset of gratitude and contentment for what you already have. Focus on appreciating the items and experiences that bring value and joy to your life, rather than constantly seeking more. Remember, embracing a clutter-free life is a personal journey, and it may take time to fully transition into this new way of living. Be patient with yourself and celebrate the progress you make along the way. Surround yourself with a supportive network of friends, family, or professional organizers who can provide guidance and encouragement when needed. By embracing a clutter-free life, you open up space for new opportunities, experiences, and personal growth. You deserve to live in an environment that supports your well-being and allows you to thrive. Embrace the journey and enjoy the many benefits that a clutter-free life has to offer.

# Conclusion

Congratulations! You have reached the end of "From Hoarder to Order: Decluttering Your Mind and Environment." Throughout this book, we have explored the complexities of hoarding disorder and provided guidance on how to overcome it. Let's take a moment to reflect on what we've learned. Hoarding disorder is a challenging mental health condition that goes beyond normal clutter or collecting. It is characterized by excessive acquisition and difficulty discarding possessions. We have discussed the signs and symptoms of hoarding disorder, as well as the consequences it can have on various aspects of a person's life. Emotionally and psychologically, hoarding disorder can lead to feelings of anxiety, guilt, shame, overwhelm, and isolation. It can strain relationships and impact the overall quality of life. Recognizing the emotional impact and seeking support is crucial for individuals with hoarding disorder. Understanding the root causes of hoarding behaviors is an essential step in the recovery process. Genetic, environmental, and psychological factors can contribute to the development of hoarding disorder. By seeking professional help and engaging in self-reflection, individuals can uncover the origins of their hoarding behaviors and work towards personal growth and healing. Building motivation for change is a crucial part of overcoming hoarding disorder. We have explored various motivations, such as improving quality of life, health and safety concerns, positive relationships, and financial freedom. Setting realistic goals, visualizing the desired outcome, and seeking support are important strategies for building motivation. Various therapeutic approaches, including

Acceptance and Commitment Therapy (ACT), Cognitive-Behavioral Therapy (CBT), and Dialectical Behavior Therapy (DBT), have been proven effective in treating hoarding disorder. These therapies address the emotional factors behind hoarding behaviors and provide valuable tools for managing emotions, enhancing decision-making, and developing healthy coping mechanisms. We have also delved into the practical aspects of decluttering your physical environment. From sorting and categorizing belongings to creating organizing systems and establishing routines, we have provided strategies for maintaining a clutter-free and functional living space. Cleaning and sanitizing are vital steps in the decluttering process, ensuring a safe and healthy environment. Addressing hoarding behaviors at their source, overcoming emotional attachments, and building healthy coping mechanisms are essential for long-term success. Developing a strong support network and seeking professional help are crucial in the recovery journey. Maintenance and relapse prevention are key in maintaining progress and a clutter-free life. To loved ones of individuals with hoarding disorder, it is important to approach conversations with empathy and understanding. Offer practical support, encourage professional help, set healthy boundaries, and practice self-care throughout the process. Remember, overcoming hoarding disorder is a journey that requires patience, commitment, and ongoing self-reflection. It is not an overnight process, but with determination and the strategies provided in this book, you can achieve a clutter-free mind and environment. As you embark on your own personal journey towards a clutter-free life, remember to be kind to yourself. Let go of perfectionism, celebrate small steps, and practice self-compassion. You are capable of change, and each decision to let go and embrace a clutter-free life is a step towards your well-being and happiness. Thank you for joining us on this journey From Hoarder to Order. May this book serve as a valuable resource and guide as you navigate your way towards a clutter-free mind and environment. Embrace the possibilities that await you and enjoy the freedom that comes with letting go.

Made in United States
Troutdale, OR
09/28/2024

23197735R00094